VGM Opportunities Series

D0208348

OPPORTUNITIES IN
SECRETARIAL
CAREERS

Blanche Ettinger

Foreword by
Susan Young
Executive Director
National Association of Executive Secretaries

VGM Career Horizons
NTC/Contemporary Publishing Group

Library of Congress Cataloging-in-Publication Data

Ettinger, Blanche.
    Opportunities in secretarial careers / Blanche Ettinger : foreword
  by Susan Young. — 3rd ed.
        p.   cm. — (VGM opportunities series)
    ISBN 0-8442-1777-8 (cloth). — ISBN 0-8442-1799-9 (pbk.)
    1. Secretaries—Vocational guidance.   I. Title.   II. Series.
  HF5547.5.E78   1999
  651.3'74'02373—dc21   99-17418
                                                                      CIP

Published by VGM Career Horizons
A division of NTC/Contemporary Publishing Group, Inc.
4255 West Touhy Avenue, Lincolnwood (Chicago), Illinois 60646-1975 U.S.A.
Copyright © 1999 by NTC/Contemporary Publishing Group, Inc.
Printed in the United States of America
International Standard Book Number: 0-8442-1777-8 (cloth)
                                                       0-8442-1799-9 (paper)

99   00   01   02   03   04   MV   18   17   16   15   14   13   12   11   10   9   8   7   6   5   4   3   2   1

CONTENTS

TABLES

ABOUT THE AUTHOR

Blanche Ettinger is a professor in the Business Department at Bronx Community College of The City University of New York and a former adjunct professor in the Business Education Program at New York University. She initially taught on the high school level; prior to that she was secretary to the executive vice president of Cohn Hall Marx Company.

She received her B.A. degree and M.S. in education from Hunter College of The City University of New York and an Ed.D. in business education from New York University, where she also took many courses in guidance and occupational information.

Dr. Ettinger has earned a national reputation for her many contributions to the field of business education. Through the years, she has been active in professional organizations and has served as president of the Business Education Association of Metropolitan New York; the New York State Association of Two-Year Colleges; Office Technology/ Secretarial Educators of SUNY; and Alpha Xi Chapter of Delta Pi Epsilon, the honorary graduate business education society. Her other professional activities are numerous and include the Executive Board of the Business Education Association of Metropolitan New York until 1998; the 1990 Awards Committee of Alpha Chapter, Delta Pi Epsilon; editor of the spring 1985, 1986, and 1987 *BEA Journal* of the Business Education Association of Metropolitan New York; editorial board member of *Educational Dimensions,* the professional journal of The New York State Association of Two-Year Colleges; PLS Certifying Board member of the National Association of Legal Secretaries; National Council Delegate of Alpha Xi Chapter, Delta Pi Epsilon; and program cochairperson of the 1986 Annual Conference of the Eastern Business Education Association. She is also a member of the Business Teachers Association, the National Business Education Association, International Society of Business Education, and Phi Delta Kappa.

The author was the recipient in 1982 of the prestigious Delta Pi Epsilon National Research Award. Other honors bestowed upon her in recognition of her leadership, scholarship, and contributions to the field of business education include: 1992 Outstanding Business Educator award of the Business Education Association of Metropolitan New York; 1987 EBEA Educator-of-the-Year; 1987 Outstanding Member Award of The New York State Association of Two-Year Colleges; 1982 Paul S. Lomax Award (Alpha Chapter, New York University); 1979 Estelle L. Popham Award (Alpha Xi Chapter, Hunter College); and 1977 Certificate of Recognition (New York State Association of Two-Year Colleges). She also is listed in *Who's Who in the East, Foremost Women of the Twentieth Century, Who's Who in American Education, Who's Who in the World,* and *Dictionary of International Biography.*

Among her recent books (some with coauthors) are *Machine Transcription: Applied Language Skills,* third edition (1999); *Medical Transcription* (1998); *Communication for the Workplace: An Integrated Language Approach* (1997); *Opportunities in Office Occupations* (1995); *Opportunities in Customer Service* (1992); *Keyboarding Proficiency Drillbook* (1988); and *Time-It! Drillbook* (1988). *Communication for the Workplace: An Integrated Language Approach* won the Alpha Chapter (NYU), Delta Pi Epsilon Award for the best text for the year.

In addition to writing, Dr. Ettinger is an educational consultant. She conducts workshops and is a guest speaker, moderator, or panelist at many institutions as well as at annual conventions and professional meetings throughout the nation.

FOREWORD

Few fields have evolved as extensively in recent years as that of the professional secretary or administrative assistant. The amazing technological advances of the past few years—as well as the ever-changing economic climate—have revolutionized the very core of business operations. As business executives strive to keep up with these changes and trends, their assistants are encouraged and expected to do so as well, by keeping pace with new skills, assuming higher-level tasks, and working more efficiently than ever before.

It is both a challenging and an exciting time to join this profession. Opportunities exist for good secretaries in any field that interests you: from law or medicine to manufacturing or entertainment. If you aspire to reach the very top of the profession—and have the skills and the drive to do so—you'll find an unprecedented level of responsibility, respect, and financial reward.

To succeed as an administrative assistant today, at any level, you must have more than outstanding secretarial skills. You must also be a good listener, an avid learner, a diligent worker, and a flexible organizer. You must be willing to serve in a supporting capacity, yet take pride in the invaluable service that good secretarial support provides.

Whatever your goals within the field, I encourage you to perfect your skills, work hard, and learn all you can every day on the job. Remain open-minded toward all opportunities. And above all, network with secretaries in your company, in your community, and in professional organizations to keep on top of changes, trends, opportunities, and compensation.

If you decide to pursue your career in this field, let me be among the first to welcome you to your new profession and congratulate you on the important role you will play in helping to shape the business of tomorrow.

Susan Young
Executive Director
National Association of Executive Secretaries

PREFACE

This third edition of *Opportunities in Secretarial Careers* is designed to enlighten you about the changing office environment, the employee demographics, the impact of the technological revolution on secretarial or administrative assistant positions, and projections for the future. This is an exciting time for you to be a prospective candidate for a position as an office professional. You will become familiar with the many titles now being substituted for *secretary* because of increased responsibilities and expertise contributed to the organization. Your functions not only will be much broader in scope, but the procedures you use will be based on the new technologies and their capabilities.

Searching for a job has always been a difficult task, particularly today when such dramatic changes have occurred in the workplace. You must be alert to the new jobs that are evolving and the future trends. Where will these jobs be and what kind of retraining will you need? Not only have titles changed for office personnel, but while the traditional skills of oral and written communications, organization, record keeping, time management, and interpersonal relations remain very important, new areas of expertise have surfaced that now are necessary: budgeting, project management, teamwork, problem solving, and advanced computer skills.

To plan for a satisfying and fulfilling career, you need to use an organized and systematic approach. Your first step is a self-examination. Determine what you really want to be, and then evaluate your interests, likes and dislikes, personality, abilities, and shortcomings. When you have a realistic image of yourself and understand the forces that motivate you, you are ready to begin your job search in the specialized field of your choice.

While you are still in school, gain as much knowledge and understanding about the many aspects of society and the business world. Get as much experience as you can on the computer, learn to use the Internet, and become adept at sending e-mail messages. Knowing how to use the Internet is essential in this society. You will learn to search the Internet for a job where companies post information about a position. You may even be required to develop an electronic resume, where the use of words differs. The employer may request information via e-mail to which you will respond via e-mail. The traditional resume differs in format and goal from the electronic resume, which is sent via the computer. Be prepared with the type of document you will need based on the company where you are searching for a job. Also, read in this text about the various types of preliminary interviewing procedures: by telephone, on the Internet, and on-site.

This book reflects the latest developments and trends in the secretarial profession and provides data on educational preparation, qualifications, promotional opportunities, salaries, trends, and strategies to use in the job search. If you are interested in working in Canada, the latest information available is given on the secretarial profession.

After you read this book, you should be able to make informed decisions about your future and to plan your strategies that will enable you to find a rewarding and challenging career.

ACKNOWLEDGMENTS

A special thanks to the following individuals for their invaluable comments in the creation of this book to help students bridge the gap between the academic and business world: Luther J. Avery, Janice Nicosia, Barbara G. Pollack, Manny Stein, and Sharon A. Stewart.

CHAPTER 1

THE CHANGING WORKFORCE

As professional secretaries, you need to be ready to embrace the challenge of change that has evolved during the last decade and that affects every aspect of our society: demographic shifts, changing workplace, global economy, office environment, and modes of communication. Computerization and high-tech equipment have given the workplace a new image and have altered job descriptions and responsibilities. Changes occurred at a revolutionary pace, much faster than we ever dreamed possible or experienced in previous decades. What does this mean? It means you need to prepare for the twenty-first century by becoming more skilled in using technology, software, hardware, network systems, fax machines, Internet, and e-mail. In conjunction with becoming highly skilled, you need to adopt the soft skills: good personal skills, flexibility, responsibility, and a lifelong learning attitude. Secretaries, as well as other office professionals, must understand and accept the "new world" in which they work and live and must plan their careers with all the available information about where the jobs will be in the future. Albert Einstein's statement sums it up: "Everything has changed but our ways of thinking. If we do not change these, we drift towards unparalleled catastrophe."[1]

In essence, we are living in a very different world—a global economy where the competition is keen, business relationships vary, operational modes differ, and organizations are carefully designed to meet the competition in a timely, effective manner.

---

[1]William Brock, "The Education Imperative," *Government Technology,* Special Edition (May 1998): 20.

DEMOGRAPHIC SHIFTS

People are living longer, and the elderly population is growing. The baby boomers (born from 1946 to 1964) are aging now, and they are thus no longer a deterrent in hiring older workers. James E. Challenger, president of Challenger, Gray & Christman Inc., an international outplacement firm, stated that "over the next ten years, as the average age of the American worker increases, older workers will possess two of the characteristics most prized by employers: they will be experienced and they will be affordable."[2] Within the next ten years, one of every three people over age fifty-five will be in the workforce. In January 1997, 12 percent, or 32.3 million of the 26.1 million civilian noninstitutional population, was at least sixty-five years old. The general population will continue to show an increase from the year 1996–2006.[3]

According to Howard Fullerton, Jr., in the Office of Employment Projections, Bureau of Labor Statistics, "Minority groups that have grown the fastest in the past—Asians and other (Pacific Islanders, American Indians, and Alaska Natives) and Hispanics—are projected to grow much faster than white non-Hispanics." The sixteen to twenty-four and fifty-five to sixty-four year olds will increase as part of the population during the 1996–2006 period. The massive immigration that started in the 1970s and that is continuing at a substantial rate, approximately 820,000 each year, has had a meaningful impact on the growth rates of the population. Immigration, primarily precipitated by the opportunities to find work in the United States, also affected the workforce population as the growth rate of individuals aged twenty-five to thirty-four continued to rise. Their numbers grew from 32 million in 1976 to 41.7 million in 1986 to 43.1 million in 1996.

THE AMERICAN WORKPLACE

The technology revolution and the global market are two major factors in the transformation of the workplace. Some companies restruc-

---

[2]"Workplace Shifts, Favors Over-50 Set," *The Secretary* (June/July 1996): 5.
[3]"Labor force 2006: slowing down and changing composition," *Monthly Labor Review* (November 1997): 24.

tured to maintain a focus on what can be done most productively for growth, profit, and competitive advantage. Other organizations eliminated old jobs and developed new job opportunities. As stated in the *IEE Insider,* "...the very character of the American workplace is changing—in how work is organized, in how workers are matched with jobs, and in how wages and the terms of employment are set and who has a voice in that determination."[4] This newsletter also indicated that wage inequality has grown, job stability has declined for vulnerable workers, and the chances for upward mobility have deteriorated among low-skill workers. Employees are downsized, training of entry-level employees is reduced, and the traditional paths to upward mobility are negligible. Lifetime jobs are a thing in the past, and employers rely on the market for skilled workers.

VISIONS FOR THE NEXT MILLENNIUM

The office of the next millennium will be anyplace—a home office, a hotel room, a railway station, a car. Office professionals will be highly dependent on technology as it continues to emerge and make transmission of voice, data, and images faster and less expensive. Leonard B. Kruk, president of Office Visions Consulting, Brick, NJ, believes that "new and emerging technologies will revolutionize how workers share information and make knowledge increasingly important, either in person or via electronics."[5] Video and sound will be the next two items in documents that will be able to convey more information than can the printed word alone, according to Joel Whitesel.[6] He also believes that multifunction machines will replace separate machines, and desktop computers will handle the work of a library, communications center, and information processor.

If you wish to pursue a career as an office professional, you should become aware of the projections and how new developments will impact

---

[4]"New Employment Policies for the Emerging Post-Industrial Labor Market," *IEE Insider,* Institute on Education and the Economy (June 1998): 5.

[5]Leonard B. Kruk, "FutureVisioning: Your Career for the New Millennium," *The Secretary* (January 1996): 6.

[6]Joel Whitesel, "Office Technology Evolves for the New Century," *The Secretary* (April 1996): 6.

the job. Whitesel's column included the following information: The ability to search for and retrieve information on the Internet will be a crucial skill for office personnel; more people will be using Internet e-mail instead of local network versions; voice and real-time video will accompany e-mail as communications technology advances and the bandwidth of phone and cable systems expands; live videoconferences from individual desktops will be available on computers that have digital video cameras and microphones; trackballs, glidepoints, and voice control will be used more than the mouse; and information processing will continue to be the main function of office technology.

OFFICE DESIGN FOR THE NEXT CENTURY

Mobility, relocation of work area, and flexible work arrangements are the criteria established for designing alternative offices for the twenty-first century, which will consist of furnishings, accessories, services, and programs. The purpose is to respond to employees' needs by making the workplace easy to use and giving employees technological access, the comforts of home, flexibility, and adequate space for staff interaction and changing needs. Companies that are supporting the concept of alternative offices believe that satisfied employees make good teams, which results in a better work environment and a higher level of productivity.[7]

THE U.S. ECONOMY

According to the Bureau of Labor Statistics, the economy expanded at a solid pace in 1997, with almost every sector showing improvement. The outlook until 2006 reflects the increased globalization of the economy and projects that the foreign trade sector will be the fastest-growing component of the gross domestic product. Exports and imports are projected to grow approximately three to three and a half times faster than the gross domestic product. Private investment also will have a more substantial position in the economy. The fundamental factor in the growth of foreign

---

[7]Robert Sagot, "Office Design in the 21st Century," *Office Systems 98* (June 1998): 22–23.

trade and private investment is the expanding business in high technology and computer-related products. Therefore, as an office professional in a knowledge-based economy, it is important that you develop your competencies for growth and mobility in a global economy.

EMPLOYMENT DATA

The job market for the past six years has had uninterrupted growth. In 1997, employment growth accelerated with total employment increasing by approximately 2.3 million. Women accounted for about 1.2 million of the growth from 1996 to 1997; men about 1 million. Business and health services had the greatest employment gains in 1997, ending with the fourth quarter, 5.8 and 2.3 percent, respectively.

An interesting development, which was discussed in *State Trends* of The Council of State Governments, summer 1998 issue, is the concern that some state governments have in losing skilled workers/students to other parts of the country. In essence, they fear losing in-state students to out-of-state jobs. Factors attributing to this movement might be higher wages, lower tuition, and academic reputation of out-of-state schools. To counteract this movement, some states are considering scholarships, financial aid packages, and internship programs.

Administrative Support Occupations

The category of administrative support occupations, including clerical, is projected to have an employment level of 25.5 million workers in 2006 and is expected to remain the largest major occupational group, as it was in both 1985 and 1996. Therefore, although the number of workers is expected to increase by only 1.8 million jobs, or 8 percent, from 1996 to 2006, it is a field of work to be considered. Secretarial jobs, except legal and medical, are expected to decline since this occupation is affected by technological change. However, jobs that involve a great deal of contact with people are less affected by changing technology. If you want to be a secretary, then you should develop the administrative and human relation skills in conjunction with the required computer skills so that you can assume the higher-level responsibilities expected of office professionals today.[8] Read the current job ads for an overview of titles, requirements, and firms where employment positions are available.

Multiple Positions

Multiple jobholders add millions of jobs to the economy and are significant to an analysis of the labor market. According to 1995 data of the Current Population Survey, 125 million people had primary jobs and 7.9 million had secondary jobs, which totaled 132.9 million jobs. Approximately 8 million workers, or 6.1 percent of the total number employed, held more than one job at a time in 1997. More than half combined a full-time job with a part-time one; one in five combined two part-time jobs. The percentage of women who held part-time jobs was two and a half times greater than the number of men who worked two or more part-time jobs. This led employers to redesign more flexible and innovative programs to meet the needs of contemporary family structures.[9]

An interesting factor is that the data show that the percentage of individuals holding multiple positions increased with education. Generally, wages were higher, too. However, these factors did not contribute to the reasons for working at more than one job. Besides financial reasons for multiple positions, individuals with more education may have the skills and knowledge for which employers are looking. Worthy to note is the fact that persons with a primary job do not necessarily earn more than they do on a secondary job. See Table 1 and note the average small difference of $7 that single jobholders earned. In Table 2, note that 23.4 percent of administrative support personnel worked on a similar type of secondary job.

LITERACY

The National Education Goals Report, 1997 noted that "Individuals demonstrating higher levels of literacy are more likely to be employed,

[8]George T. Silvestri, "Occupational Employment Projections to 2006," *Monthly Labor Review* (November 1997): 61.

[9]Randy E. Lig and Angela Clinton, "Strong Job Growth Continues, Unemployment Declines in 1997," *Monthly Labor Review* (February 1998): 48–61.

Table 1. COMPARISON OF SINGLE AND MULTIPLE JOBHOLDERS BY MEDIAN EARNINGS AND OCCUPATIONAL GROUP OF PRIMARY JOBS

Occupational group of primary job	Number of multiple jobholders	Percent	Median primary job earnings		
			Single jobholders	Multiple jobholders	Dollar difference
Total employed	7,924	6.3	$407	$400	$7
Executive, administrative, and managerial	1,072	6.2	659	607	52
Professional specialty	1,648	9.1	654	604	50
Technicians and related support	301	7.7	511	456	55
Sales	867	5.7	322	285	37
Administrative support, including clerical	1,188	6.5	354	325	29
Private household workers	51	6.1	130	161	–31
Service workers, except private household	1,152	7.1	228	268	–40
Farming, forestry, and fishing	191	5.2	256	296	–40
Precision production, craft, and repair	688	4.7	507	506	1
Machine operators, assemblers, and inspectors	327	4.1	352	381	–29
Transportation and material moving occupations	263	5.1	434	366	68
Handlers, equipment cleaners, helpers, and laborers	230	4.6	277	277	0.0

Source: *Monthly Labor Review*, March 1997, p. 10.

Table 2. DISTRIBUTION OF THE SECONDARY JOBS OF MULTIPLE JOBHOLDERS BY OCCUPATIONAL GROUP OF PRIMARY JOB AND EMPLOYMENT IN SECONDARY JOBS BY OCCUPATIONAL GROUP

Occupation of primary job	Total employed (thousands)		Occupation of secondary job				
	Number	Percent	Executive, administrative, and managerial	Professional specialty	Technician and related support	Sales	Administrative support
Total employed	7,413	100.0	9.7	20.3	2.5	17.9	9.7
Executive, administrative, and managerial	1,024	100.0	22.2	18.8	1.7	22.0	10.1
Professional specialty	1,540	100.0	9.5	53.3	2.2	11.6	5.6
Technician and related support	281	100.0	7.2	14.5	25.7	14.9	10.7
Sales	833	100.0	10.9	14.5	0.9	28.0	10.0
Administrative support	1,119	100.0	6.7	10.4	1.3	26.6	23.4
Private household	41	100.0	1.9	7.3	0.0	9.3	14.6
Service, except private household	1,063	100.0	5.0	8.0	2.0	13.0	6.2
Farming, forestry, and fishing	168	100.0	8.1	7.4	0.9	12.4	9.9
Precision production, craft, and repair	597	100.0	9.5	10.6	1.2	14.6	3.3
Machine operators, assemblers, and inspectors	300	100.0	4.6	7.5	1.5	14.5	5.2
Transportation and material moving	230	100.0	6.0	5.4	1.0	11.8	5.1
Handlers, equipment handlers, and laborers	217	100.0	2.9	6.6	2.0	13.3	7.1
Number of secondary jobs	7,413		719	1,504	187	1,325	717
Percent additional jobs			4.0	7.7	4.6	8.1	3.8

Source: *Monthly Labor Review*, March 1997, p. 13.

work more weeks in a year, and earn higher wages than individuals demonstrating low levels of literacy." The report states that high school students with a diploma or less need to take additional instruction in adult education to upgrade their skills and qualify for better jobs. People need to be able to speak, write, read, solve problems, understand maps and read street signs, read bus schedules, etc.

THE CANADIAN ECONOMY AND WORKFORCE

Strengthened by merchandise exports and a buildup of inventories, the Gross Domestic Products grew by 4.2 percent at an annual rate in the fourth quarter of 1997, according to the April 1998 *Canada Quarterly* from the Canadian Embassy in Washington, DC. Growth for the entire year of 1997 was 3.8 percent, which equaled the U.S. rate. The unemployment rate dropped from 8.5 percent in March 1998 to 8.4 percent in April. Two-way trade of goods, services, and income on investments between Canada and the United States went up by more than 12 percent. Canada has experienced much success and growth in environmental, telecommunications, and information technologies. Teleglobe, the Canadian international network operator, is moving into retail telephone services. "The company's strategy is to be among the top three in the international telecommunications market," as stated in the summer 1998 issue of *News & Arts* from the Canadian Consulate General.

As a result of significant investments in services, technology, equipment, and new methods of production, the Canadian economy, like that of the United States, is undergoing tremendous changes. Also, like most economically advanced countries, the fastest, most remarkable growth has been in the service sector, which accounts for the largest number of jobs and a shortage of flexible, skilled workers. Taking into account the entire population employed in retail and wholesale trade, finance, and transportation, as well as public and federal service employees, approximately two-thirds of all Canadians are employed in the service sector. Currently women comprise 49.5 percent of the workforce, and almost a quarter of all employees in the executive category are women—23 percent—up from 21.3 percent in March 1996. In the administrative support occupational category of the public service sector, there were 63,282 employees of which 52,904, or 83.6 percent were women. Overall employment in office occupations is expected to show little growth and may even see a slight decline; however, employment growth is expected in areas such as professional business services, private law practices, hospitals, and medical laboratories.

CHAPTER 2

NATURE OF SECRETARIAL/OFFICE PROFESSIONAL POSITIONS

The opportunities for secretarial careers continue to grow and offer a bright future. They are the largest segment of the office workforce: 3,349,000 people are employed as secretaries and administrative specialists. According to the U.S. Department of Labor, approximately 400,000 new secretarial jobs will be added by the year 2005. Jobs will be plentiful for the generalist, especially for well-qualified and experienced secretaries who replace retired workers and those who relocate. Several new rapidly growing industries—personnel supply, management and public relations, and computer and data processing—will also generate jobs. For the specialists, with the health services industry growing at a faster than average pace, medical secretaries will be able to be selective; with the expansion of the legal services profession, legal secretaries are presently and will continue to be in demand.

The revolution in office technology and computerization has led to changing roles of secretaries. They have assumed higher-level responsibilities and have become more productive as they learned to handle computers, voice message systems, fax machines, e-mail, and scanners. Also, with corporate and workforce restructuring, administrative duties have been altered, expanded, or reassigned. If this occurs when you are a secretary, stay calm, set goals, determine what skills you need to know, and get the training needed to assume your new responsibilities. William Ayers, president of Ayers Group, recommends that you keep in mind that "restructuring can be a positive experience. It will give you a chance to explore new areas and develop new skills."[1] You will find that your work will become more rewarding and challenging.

Administrative staff frequently are the office's most knowledgeable people when using computer software to do word processing, presentations, and spreadsheets. Gerri Kozlowski, CPS, 1977–98 International President of Professional Secretaries International, stated that "Expertise in computer software is a major asset the administrative professional brings to the office. This tool has given administrative staff the capability to process and manage a broad range of information."

In the past, secretaries generally worked for one individual or in a pool. In today's workforce, managers and professionals share secretaries. However, presidents of corporations, partners of legal firms, and CEOs still require a highly skilled secretary to perform the responsibilities of the position. A recent poll by Professional Secretaries International revealed that 60 percent of secretaries said they now report to more than one boss, with 20 percent saying they report to four or more.[2] The team concept has been accepted in many offices.

If you are considering a secretarial career, then you should be aware of trends that are affecting the nature of the work and the competencies required for positions in automated offices. Although our highly technological and competitive world will continue to expand bringing about further changes in the work environment, set your goals not only for mastery of the technical skills but for the personal, administrative, communicative, and interactive skills that cannot be replaced by equipment. Nancy Freeze, a marketing assistant at Hewlett-Packard and president of the San Jose chapter of Professional Secretaries International, clearly supports the previous comment when she responded "absolutely no" to the statement that secretaries could be replaced by the tools now available. For example, why should an executive have to spend time responding to the 20 percent of voice mail and e-mail messages that are junk. How can software understand office politics and bring important infor-

---

[1]William L. Ayers, "Coping with Job Restructuring," *Beyond Computing* (July/August 1998): 10.

[2]Alan Farnham, "Where Have All the Secretaries Gone?" *Fortune* (May 12, 1997): 153–154.

mation to the manager's attention? The technology could never rival the sophisticated judgment of a human secretary.

In Canada, office automation is redefining the role of the secretary into that of information worker. The growth of the service industry, technological innovation, and changing procedures are transforming both the nature of jobs and the skills required to do them. Employers are now seeking employees with the following competencies: computer expertise, knowledge of word processing software packages, ability to transcribe documents, basic academic competence, analytical and problem-solving abilities, communication and interpersonal skills, initiative, creativity, and adaptability.

FROM SECRETARIES TO MANAGERS

The professional secretary has become a part of the management team. Secretaries no longer handle just the routine duties of keyboarding, filing, and copying but have become decision makers and provide the links between the different parts of the organization. They are increasingly handling tasks previously performed by managers and other professionals. In fact, secretaries are the first employees who are asked to assume the tasks once handled by displaced middle managers, which include everything from drafting contracts to running spreadsheets to solving customer problems. Today's secretary is a goal-oriented manager. New attitudes and expectations on the part of both secretary and management are evolving. Below are several managerial roles frequently filled by secretaries:[3]

- Information Manager—handles paper records and the organization's electronic files and databases; develops methods for organizing and retrieving records
- Communications Manager—writes and edits
- Inventory Manager— monitors inventory levels and condition of equipment and develops specifications for purchase of products

---

[3]Richard G. Ensman, "Today's Secretaries, Today's Managers," *The Secretary* (June/July 1995): 15–16.

- Planning Manager—keeps tabs on details relating to projects
- Logistics Manager—handles travel, meeting schedules, and agendas
- Policy Manager—maintains company manual and interprets policies and procedures to employees
- Employee Relations Manager—interviews and hires and acts as supervisor to less-senior staff
- Financial Manager—prepares and approves vouchers and financial correspondence
- Community Relations Manager—solves customer needs and problems
- Training Manager—provides guidance on workplace skills
- Action Manager—organizes the boss's workload

MOBILITY

Many career paths are being created for persons in office/administrative professions. For ambitious individuals, a secretarial position is a stepping-stone to a higher-level job. Advancement generally is by promotion to a secretarial position that has more responsibility. Qualified secretaries who have gained a broad knowledge of the company's operations and have enhanced their skills may be given higher positions such as senior or executive secretary, office manager, or clerical supervisor. In some instances, qualified secretaries who have a business acumen can advance to training, supervisory, and managerial jobs. They may also receive a job in desktop publishing, information management and research, instructor or sales representative with manufacturers of software or computer equipment.

Secretaries have become invaluable to some employers who are reluctant to show approval of a promotion because they don't want to lose their secretaries who frequently are their confidantes and someone to bounce things off of. A director of a museum stated, "Just for the sheer volume of information and knowledge of the running of the museum, the history of the museum, and the thousands of people involved in making the museum go, she is invaluable."

Developments in office technology will definitely continue at an astonishing pace and will further change the secretary's work environment. New technical terms indicative of the kind of work performed in a modern office are being added to those that have been around for a while, such as integration, cyberspace, networked office, multimedia, infrastructure, web site, NT server, audio- and videoconferencing, browser, search engines, and digital communication. As new systems and modes of operation occur, new titles will emerge reflecting the higher levels of skills necessitated by the changing nature of the job. Currently, secretaries are known by different designations, too, which reflect the increased responsibilities assumed in the office.

VIEWPOINTS OF SECRETARIAL PROFESSIONALS

Viewpoints from various experienced professionals in the field on the expanding, multifaceted role of the secretary are presented here to give interested individuals a better understanding of secretarial work as a career. Through their statements run a common understanding that as secretarial positions become more challenging, secretaries are taking on bigger roles; they are assuming higher-level decision-making responsibilities, which are reflected in the new titles that are evolving. Education beyond high school in computers, oral presentation, and written skills is becoming a prerequisite for advancement.

Susan Skarness, Certified Professional Secretary (CPS), executive assistant to the senior vice president and vice president in the corporate development department of Enron Corporation, one of the largest natural gas and electricity companies, states that, "The secretarial career is one of the most exciting careers in business." She believes that continuing education is most important and can be achieved by attendance at workshops and seminars, enrollment at local schools and universities, and by networking at meetings of Professional Secretaries International.

Sharon A. Stewart, administrative secretary at Sidney Rubell Co., a real estate firm, was hired seventeen years ago. She still remembers that Mr. Rubell told her she would learn many things on the job, and the most complex facet would be about people. After many years of experience, Ms. Stewart supports that statement and says, "He did not exaggerate!"

> When I was hired in August 1981, I came to New York from California and was uncertain if I wanted to remain in New York. I never left. My advice to you is to work hard and develop good skills so that you will not feel threatened.

The most striking difference between then and now is the manual office. The bookkeeping, record keeping, ledgers, rent bills, invoices, etc., were all done by hand. No computers, no fax machine, no answering machine, and no backup. Just me! Looking back, I am amazed that it all got done.

If you are interested in this field and want to be successful on the job, you must be prepared and know how to manage your time. Time management is invaluable, and knowing how to prioritize is the ultimate office tool.

I have always considered myself a professional. I have always tried to conduct myself in a courteous and professional manner, whether in dealings with my boss, the tenants, or the plumber. Although I am basically a secretary, at times I also have had to be a diplomat, a referee, and even the scapegoat.

A good experience on a job will result in growth of knowledge and enhancement of capabilities. To a company, you are an asset and are contributing to its productivity. Make your job a continuous learning experience.

Barbara G. Pollack, a recently retired business education teacher, was the occupational education chairperson from 1981 to 1995 at Hendrick Hudson High School, Montrose, New York. After retirement, she decided to apply her knowledge to a career in the business world, which has given her very broad experiences with major companies such as IBM, Con Edison, and Citibank. She believes individuals interested in secretarial careers must keep up with the changing office trends, especially by learning the computer and various software programs. Another very good way to remain up to date is to work as an office temp employee in the corporate world. The statements below come from her wealth of experience in a wide range of employment activities.

If you plan to work for a temporary agency, have a resume ready to submit to them and be prepared to take tests that may be in keyboarding, grammar, math, or computer operations. Major temporary employment agencies may even have self-paced software to train you on various software programs. If you score very well on the test after training, the agency might get a trainer for you so that you can continue learning the equipment to apply for a higher-level job. In addition to the skills, the agencies will send you out frequently for a job if you dress in corporate business attire, have the common sense of maturity, and possess advanced computer skills.

In large corporations, be prepared to be approached to orient new employees to the job. Write everything down when you get *your* orientation. Then write a job description with how-to's to share with the permanent employees so that they can carry out their duties without excessive questioning. Familiarize yourself with the organization chart of the department in which you work and have a place for important phone numbers, the code for the department, and the names of persons with whom you have contact.

When a filing system doesn't exist, assume the responsibility and set up the filing cabinets in a systematic way. Learn how to produce labels on your computer and set up a system for labeling documents with a code in a smaller font size at the bottom of the last page of the document you are producing.

Keep your workstation neat; put things away each evening; learn how your manager wants work returned for signature; learn how to pick up documents after your superior has looked at them and marked them for distribution, filing, or calendaring. Mark each change as you learn of it with a colored pen; then correct the calendar on the computer at the end of the day. Print a copy of each calendar for yourself as well as the manager.

Become familiar with the phone system in your company, particularly transferring calls. Find out from your manager whether he/she prefers that you send them on or screen them first. Remember to learn the names of all your superiors, get coverage for your phone when you step away, or program it for your "voice mailbox." Smile before picking up the receiver to sound pleasant.

Take advantage of all in-service training. If your company pays for college courses, take them. Join the local professional organizations to network with others. That way, you will be on the cutting edge and are more valuable to your organization. On the job, you need to score as close as possible to 100 percent accuracy for everything you do. It is a good idea to team up with a coworker, if possible. Be friendly to everyone, and learn about your community to be prepared for setting up an outside luncheon or to direct a visitor to your office from the train, plane, or highway.

These statements reflect the need for secretaries who are challenged and who will be able to cope with the higher-level responsibilities that require thinking individuals who can make decisions, manage and execute projects, manipulate and manage information, and enhance office operations. Undoubtedly, secretaries with the appropriate background, skills, knowledge, and motivation to learn will have many career opportunities in the years ahead.

The scope of this book is to give you a comprehensive overview of the secretarial profession so that you will have a greater understanding of this career and the labor market.

HISTORICAL GROWTH OF PROFESSIONAL SECRETARIES

To understand the modern role of the professional secretary, it is necessary to trace the evolution of the office. An understanding of the past coupled with the present will give you a better grasp of what is yet to come.

The earliest civilizations of Greece had need for secretaries (also known as confidants) to handle the correspondence and to record historical, business, private, and public information. Shorthand was mastered by such Roman leaders as Julius Caesar and the Emperor Augustus. In Italy and in France, it was used until the seventh century A.D., when it became mistrusted and disappeared into the cloisters during the Middle Ages. During the period of the Renaissance, from 1400 to 1500, several shorthand systems were developed in England, initially with religious terms, to be followed by legal, political, and finally commercial words. In the early days in the United States, in contrast to the current female-dominated secretarial positions, men dominated the office, performing stenographic and bookkeeping tasks. This was considered a position with distinction and status and from which these men could be elevated to higher positions. "Personal" or "private" preceded the word secretary to reflect this status. In the United States, John Quincy Adams, Henry Adams, John Hay, and Lyndon Johnson were some of our great leaders who began their careers as secretaries to important political persons.

It was not until Christopher Sholes invented the typewriter in 1867 and perfected it in 1873 that shorthand increased in use. Together, they became communication tools. About this time, women very slowly began to enter the office in stenographic positions, and private business schools began to flourish. Contrary to current statistics, which indicate a large enrollment of women, originally men and boys were students. It wasn't until the beginning of the twentieth century that the majority of trainees were women.

Another item of interest is that when men were working as private secretaries, the position was a prestigious one, but as soon as women began to assume this role, a reversal in image occurred. There was obvious discrimination against women, for they received much less pay than men for the same long hours. They were expected to conduct themselves properly and with loyalty. Women filled the void created by the expansion of industry and the growth of paperwork. They adapted to the technology of the time and learned how to operate the typewriter, telephone, transcribing machines, and calculation machines.

By the 1930s, women dominated the office workforce and once again kept pace with technology by learning the electric typewriter. A small group of women who had foresight and vision recognized the importance of continuing education and became the charter members of the Professional Secretaries International (originally the National Secretaries Association), organized in 1942. In Chapter 5, you will read about the Institute for Certifying Secretaries, a group responsible for a certifying examination for secretaries, which was designed in 1951.

The next major breakthrough occurred in the mid-1960s with the introduction by IBM (International Business Machines Corporation) of the Magnetic Tape Selectric Typewriter (MT/ST). Automatic deletion and insertion of words, storage, and flawless and random access printing became a reality. This was the beginning of our modern concept of word processing. Some subsequent inventions that impacted secretarial positions were the IBM Mag Card in 1973, memory typewriters, stand-alone word processors, video display terminals, microprocessing and telecommunications technology, desktop computers, modems, optical character readers, networked systems, and integrated information systems. The introduction of advanced technology led to transformations in the office—structures, organization, position responsibilities, and working environments.

In the information era of the 1990s, office environments were changing very rapidly, and secretaries, once again, had to meet the challenges of the new explosion of technology. Personal computers were appearing on desks of executives, secretaries, and other office support staff in both large and small offices.

The new generation of computer technology enhanced the flow of information and processed data at much faster speeds. Greater responsibilities imposed on secretaries were the maintenance of databases, development of spreadsheets, integration of text and graphics to produce professional-looking documents, and preparation of presentation graphics, including charts, that were attractive and dramatic. Software has become more sophisticated. In the last half of the 1990s, the Internet, World Wide Web, and videoconferencing became important business and household tools. Tremendous numbers of people are in front of a keyboard—some for extended periods of time, particularly when they go into chat rooms or do research. This factor certainly supports the need to be efficient at the keyboard.

Most interesting is the research occurring presently to develop sophisticated voice output devices that would enable the computer to recognize the user's voice. Many systems are being used but need more sophistication in understanding dialects and pronunciation. The system must be highly responsive to different voices. Several speech recognition systems are now available that "know" 30,000 words. Hundreds of thousands of people use voice recognition when they place a call and respond to the recorded voice!

Research is still being done on discrete speech input, which requires the user to pause between words, and the natural speech input, which allows the person to talk in any manner.

Can you imagine what tomorrow will bring? Secretaries will continue to forge ahead and meet the challenge that they have in the past.

PROFESSIONAL SECRETARIES WEEK

Professional Secretaries Week was originated in 1952 by Professional Secretaries International with a proclamation by Charles Sawyer, Secretary of Commerce. The purpose of this forward-looking group was to uplift the image of the secretary from one of servitude to recognition of "the American secretary upon whose skills, loyalty, and efficiency the functions of business and government offices depend." Currently, the purpose of Professional Secretaries Week, which is observed annually the last full week in April, is twofold: "to increase public awareness of the vital role played by secretaries in business, industry, education, government, and the professions; and to reaffirm the dedication of secretaries to professional performance of their responsibilities." During this week, local chapters sponsor seminars and workshops while some members speak to educational, professional, and civic groups. Noted governmental officials have acknowledged the valuable contributions of professional secretaries.

In 1997, President Clinton wrote: "...Secretaries and administrative assistants play a vital role in the success of our nation.... The ongoing revolution in technology offers your profession both new challenges and new opportunities. I commend secretaries and administrative professionals across America and around the world for mastering the latest equipment and information technology to carry out your many and varied responsibilities more effectively." The prime minister of Canada, Jean Chretien, stated, "...Professional Secretaries International, by encouraging personal fulfillment and promoting career development in a global context, shows us the success of a collective effort for a common good. As you reflect on the achievements of the past year and set new objectives for the future, I am sure that you will enjoy this opportunity to reaffirm your commitment to excellence in administrative support."

In observance of Professional Secretaries Week, Elnar G. Hickman, past president of Professional Secretaries International, believed this was an appropriate time to "rededicate ourselves to proclaiming the tremendous potential a secretarial career offers." She believes that "...the secretarial profession is a way to make a living, a way to make a life, and a way to make a difference." Yes, Professional Secretaries Week is a time to show respect and recognition. Secretaries would like to see this week of recognition change from an occasion for lunch with the boss or a bouquet of flowers to an increase in responsibilities and activities as part of the management team.

QUALITY OF EMPLOYEES

Quality improvement, a concept always related to the production process, is now becoming important in white-collar work throughout the nation. The application of this concept to knowledge jobs, such as that of the secretary, was practiced by the Japanese for several decades before it was finally adopted by the United States to maintain its competitive edge against the foreign markets. Companies that are adopting such programs are involving all office employees in their search for ways to improve quality of process. Knowledge workers become aware that the task they perform is part of a total process that serves the customer. They are becoming involved in quality circles where they discuss problems, brainstorm for innovative techniques that benefit both the company and themselves, make decisions, and interrelate with their peers.

REACHING OUT TO BE HEARD

Men were the first secretaries. They were highly regarded and often promoted to prestigious positions as private and personal secretaries. Women began to make inroads with the invention of the typewriter and the era of the Industrial Revolution. Gradually, the majority of men retired from this field. Women, the new entrants as secretaries, realized they weren't accorded the same status as the men were given. As stated in the previous section, the women collaborated and organized the National Secretaries Association in 1942. This organization was the initial feminist's voice of secretaries reaching out to business and industry. However, it was not until the women's liberation movement started in the 1960s as well as other publicized provocative activities, such as *The Secretarial Ghetto* written by Mary Kathleen Benet and the film *9 to 5,* that a new breed of secretary evolved and consciousness raising among secretaries was activated.

Those secretaries who have assumed managerial responsibilities such as budget management or who perform the higher-level tasks associated with spreadsheeting, database management, graphics design, and presentation visuals want to be recognized, rewarded, and viewed as a vital part of the team. These "high-tech" skills, sometimes in combination with "high-touch" skills, are often unnoticed. One interviewer of ward secretaries at a university teaching hospital revealed that although the responsibilities for "coordinating and organizing patient-care information through the use of a computerized record system" were recognized in job evaluations, the equally important human relations skills involving the use of diplomacy in "coordinating and organizing people, patients, and medical personnel" went unrecognized.

Secretaries are clearly making their voices heard to be recognized, to be given increased responsibilities, and to be challenged with higher-level projects that would lead to upward mobility. Other secretaries are no longer content to work with somebody else's ideas and want to have greater decision-making powers as part of management.

Generally, secretaries now have more education than in previous decades, are more aware and have a greater understanding of organizational policy, and know what it means to be a professional. This has led to political activism among many women, and professional organizations help support and publicize their causes.

CHAPTER 3

ORGANIZATIONAL STRUCTURE
AND CLIMATE

Secretaries make decisions about employment opportunities based on the job itself, the organizational structure, and the physical environment. Changes have occurred in each of these areas due to increased competition that forced business restructuring or downsizing.

Workplace trends that have emerged in the last decade have stimulated conversions in the organizational structure, office environment, and ways in which office workers perform their jobs. In this chapter you will become familiar with the changing character of the modern office and the new work culture that flourished, resulting from advanced and highly sophisticated technology, innovative business practices, and alternative work styles that have impacted the role of the secretary.

Computers, originally basic tools for word processing, have now evolved into sophisticated pieces of equipment that handle multitasking and incorporate programs such as database management, spreadsheets that perform mathematical calculations, and graphics to create artwork in many forms, including data and words. Most important, computers have also evolved into communication tools that are an integral part of both small and large businesses. The technology has changed the attitudes of office staff and the way in which many tasks are performed. Modems and cellular phones have virtually turned every environment into work space.

In conjunction with the trends mentioned above, the emphasis can no longer be solely on automating corporate headquarters but rather on the virtual office, which might be a home office or a mobile office where work is performed. Companies must also recognize the need for private space in which individuals can read and think to accomplish tasks as well as a place where employees can team up with their colleagues for discussions and decision making. To achieve this, an open plan of office design can be used where partitions used are movable and acoustical screens are dividers. The individual employees' workstations are also self-contained. Fallon-McElligott refers to the "cave and commons" design to balance individual work and teamwork, privacy and community. One way of achieving this is to be able to move office furniture equipped with a computer, files, and phone into "flexible" space that can be adjusted to serve different numbers of employees. Another alternative, referred to as *hoteling,* is to provide buildings where offices or meeting rooms can be reserved.[1]

Retraining at all occupational levels, as well as continuing education, is necessary for the secretary to cope with the changing complexion of the office and to develop the ability to identify and solve problems arising from differences in the workforce. The secretarial body of knowledge has expanded tremendously; therefore, increased opportunities for upward mobility will be available only to individuals who make the effort to become broadly educated and acquire the skills and personal qualities necessary to function as a valued member of the company.

OFFICE INFORMATION SYSTEMS

The Past and Future

The past thirty years have shown dramatic changes in office technology. The electric typewriter was introduced in the early 1960s, which was a godsend to typists because of the ease and speed in keying correspondence. The memory typewriter that had the facility of self-correction came next, and by 1972, information was stored on magnetic tapes. Magnetic card equipment followed, which enabled typists to transfer information from the keyboard to a thin magnetic card for storage. The information on the card could be played back with the typed information appearing on paper. Dictaphone dictating equipment was introduced in

---

[1]Fallon Mc-Elligott, "The New Workplace," *Business Week* (April 29, 1996): 108–109.

office environments, and both word processors and centralized systems were used to transcribe this information. Word processing had its origin during the 1970s, and titles were beginning to change to *word processing specialists* rather than *typists* or *secretaries* for individuals working on this automated equipment. Three types of office configurations were used in the past to increase productivity and improve communications: 1. the centralized structure to handle heavy jobs; 2. decentralized arrangement, also referred to as satellite stations and minicenters, to support a department or selected principals; and 3. traditional one-to-one relationship between secretary and employer. However, as the cost of computers dropped in price, they were placed on individual workstations and are now commonplace. Organizations have moved to the accepted standard that is one personal computer for each office employee. With the increased responsibilities and nature of the workload, secretaries are dependent on modern technology to be productive employees.

The office environment that has emerged is different from that in the past. The explosion of technology and systems has and continues to be so rapid that even prognosticators are uncertain of future directions. What does appear to be obvious with the introduction of the palmtop computer is that computers will become miniaturized and will have all of the component parts that now exist. Different voices and handwriting will be recognized by computers, and communication via the computer will be widespread.

Other changes that are influencing the office environment pertain to roles and titles of secretaries.

Features of Office Information Systems

Office information systems are designed to improve the effectiveness of an organization by automating routine procedures, maintaining good records, facilitating communications, and offering timely customer services. These information systems are primarily computerized and vary depending on the basic needs of the company and the staff receiving support. Word processing, databases, spreadsheets, calendaring, desktop publishing, records management, and e-mail are basic components of these office information systems. Groupware is a more recent trend that enables employees to collaborate on projects.

Other subsystems of office information systems are transaction processing systems, (maintain records of all transactions); management information systems, or MIS (generate reports from data of transaction processing system); and decision support systems, or DSS (manipulate data pertinent to problems for decision making).

As stated previously, in typical organizations there is one personal computer for each office employee. Secretaries, supervisors, managers, and executives are dependent on office automation to perform their tasks. Large corporations are also moving ahead at dizzying speeds to create integrated, networked systems. As a secretary you will need to keep abreast of the latest technology. The definition of terms that follow should help you understand systems.

Applications software. Software that enables the user to perform specific tasks on the computer, i.e., word processing, spreadsheets, desktop publishing, and personal information management.

Calendaring. Keeps track of meetings and special events on a computer calendar.

Cellular phone. Enables user to have a two-way conversation from a location that is remote from the traditional office; has become very popular for many purposes—business, family responsibilities while at work, and speedily transmitting important information.

Computer program. A set of detailed instructions that enables a computer to perform a task.

Cyberspace. A computer-generated mental image of a computer world.

Database. A collection of systematically organized data or information that is stored and retrieved for various purposes.

Desktop publishing. The ability to combine text and graphics to produce reports, brochures, newsletters, and other publications of nearly the same quality as those produced by commercial print shops.

Electronic mail. Computerized information sent over telephone wires, cables, or satellites

E-mail. A message is sent electronically from one user to another.

Groupware. Software designed to help people collaborate on projects.

Internet. A collection of networks linked together around the world to exchange data and distribute processing tasks. *Intranet.* A private network in a company that enables employees to access the Internet. *Extranet.* An Intranet environment that has controlled access for public users such as authorized customers and vendors.

Multitasking. A process where you run two or more programs at a time.

Multimedia. The integrated use of computer-based media, including graphics, sound, animation, video, and images.

Netiquette. Rules of etiquette when using the Internet.

Network. Interconnection of a number of computers by communication facilities. *Local Area Network (LAN).* A computer communications network over a limited geographic area that provides for communication and sharing of resources, software, and hardware between many computer users. *Wide Area Network (WAN).* A network that spans a wide geographic area and connects two or more LANs.

Pager. Device that enables callers to contact individuals to alert them to call the number appearing on the beeper to receive a message. This device is popular with office executives and employees who are frequently away from the office.

Spreadsheet. An intersecting grid of rows and columns for the purpose of presenting numerical information and formulas in a matrix of cells. The electronic spreadsheet that is used with personal computers resembles the accountant's work sheet.

Telecommunications. An electronic method for communicating messages over telephone lines.

Windowing. A function that splits the screen into two or more parts, allowing information from another document to be displayed.

World Wide Web. A service on the Internet that is a source of information presented in a well-organized and accessible format.

TITLES OF SECRETARIAL PERSONNEL

In the past, individuals working in an office were known as receptionists, clerks, or secretaries (general, executive, legal, or medical). They generally used typewriters, transcribing machines, and duplicators to perform their tasks. The usual responsibilities included typewriting, filing, and duplicating. Indicative of the changes in technology is the low usage rate of typewriters by secretaries. In 1997, a survey showed that only 20.2 percent of the secretaries used typewriters daily compared to 51.3 percent in 1992. Although the titles of these office employees may still be used, the position has changed as well as the nature of the job. Secretaries have become much more productive since computers, fax machines, scanners, and e-mail arrived. However, there are many duties of the position that are of a personal nature and cannot be automated, such as working with clients and planning meetings and conferences.

Some titles used today are secretary, executive assistant, executive secretary, administrative secretary, administrative assistant, and office manager. A recent study of more than eight hundred members of Professional Secretaries International found that fewer than half the administrative professionals carry the word "secretary" in their titles. From 55.1 percent in 1992, the inclusion of "secretary" in the title dropped to 41 percent. In contrast to this drop, the titles "administrative assistant" and "executive assistant" rose to 31.6 percent from 13.4 percent during the same period. Other titles in the survey, which equaled 27.4 percent, included "coordinator," "administrator," "technician," "associate," and "office manager." See Table 3.[2]

Gerri Kozlowski, international president of PSI, remarked that "the shift of job titles indicates a desire among both administrative professionals and their employers to recognize administrative staff for carrying greater job responsibilities."[3]

Table 3. SECRETARIAL TITLES

Administrative Secretary	8.6%	
Secretary	18.1%	
Executive Secretary	14.3%	41.0%
Administrative Assistant	23.0%	
Executive Assistant	8.6%	31.6%

---

[2]Gerri Kozlowski, "Secretaries Sharpen Skills While Gaining New Job Titles," Professional Secretaries Association, http//www.psi.org/news-8.html, 7/9/98.
[3]Ibid.

When you search for a career, carefully determine the knowledge you will need as well as the personal qualities and technical skills that are required. When using the "Help Wanted" section of *The New York Times,* look under the various categories where you might find a job listing.

MODERN OFFICE TECHNOLOGY

The impact of technology on the office environment is apparent in the way work is performed, where it is done, how information is accessed, how computer-generated information is transported, and how communications are exchanged. New equipment and systems to increase productivity and reduce costs have been introduced; new services and strategies have been developed; and new positions have evolved. Other major changes occurred with the restructuring of the organization and downsizing, which did affect the worker and the workplace. In the next decade, predictions reveal that downsizing will continue, some permanent employees will be replaced by outsourcing (see p. 48), and the technology will continue at a tremendous rate of speed.

The driving forces behind most of these changes are the computer, the ever-increasing power of the microchip, and telecommunications. You need to be computer literate, be knowledgeable about software and hardware, understand communications systems and workplace organization, and be familiar with procedures and the office environment as you plan your secretarial career in information systems. The very nature of the job has been transformed by the information technology. You should also be aware of predictions for office information systems and management techniques that will further alter secretarial careers. The way in which you perform duties will continue to change, and technology will be the tool. An information revolution has impacted the U.S. economy. According to Linda Austin and Cheryl Willis, approximately 60 percent of today's workforce is characterized as information workers. "An information worker will be hard to distinguish from a noninformation worker in the future because information technology will have spread across the spectrum of workplaces."[4] Electronics has been and

---

[4]Linda J. Austin and Cheryl L. Willis, "Future Work," *The Changing Dimensions of Business Education,* National Business Education Yearbook, 35 (1997): 161.

will continue to be the key factor in the creation of such a mind-boggling environment, which only yesterday was considered a fantasy.

The 1980s were known as the decade of information processing, and by 1990, more than forty million people were operating video display terminals (VDTs) on their jobs. Presently there has been a great leap in computing power, resulting from advances in semiconductor chips, and these advances will undoubtedly continue. Imagine the impact of new technology on the automated office and the radical changes that are yet to come!

The categories of modern equipment found in the office that impact secretarial positions are described below:

- Stand-alone word processors—Computer equipment that enables user to input and manipulate text of all types, including hyphenation, moving and copying information, and handling merging operations.
- Communicating stand-alones—Computers that can exchange information with other computers over telephone lines.
- Dictating equipment—Units that are portable, desktop, or centralized recording systems and into which correspondence, reports, and other information are dictated.

   Digital dictation systems are a fairly new development. These systems convert a dictator's voice to digital signals, which are different from the analog recording systems described above. On a digital dictation system, the dictated document actually becomes a voice file, similar to a data file in a computer. One major advantage is that the dictator can add or delete information without recording over any material. Within the next five to ten years, digital technology will probably become commonplace.

- Transcribing machines—Voice recognition systems recognize speech patterns of individuals and translate them into printed words on a computer screen. Presently these systems are used in special areas where the dictator needs to use both hands to perform a function and therefore cannot switch on the dictation equipment. Undoubtedly, eventually these systems will be adopted by a more widespread population. What does this mean for the secretary? Although the dictated material does not have to be transcribed, it will still have to be edited carefully.
- Reprographic equipment—Image processing includes optical character recognition equipment (scanners) and desktop publishing.

Copies from image processing are made directly from originals in contrast to copies that are reproduced from masters.

A scanner is equipment that converts text or images into computer readable form. Looking ahead, the standard copier technology used at present will become digitized.

- Fax machine—Equipment that transmits text or scanned images electronically over telephone lines.
- Microcomputers (personal computers)—Computer technology has already moved to the secretary's desk as well as the executive's. Presently, each office employee has a computer terminal. Software programs give these machines information processing capabilities, such as word processing, accounting spreadsheets, graphic designs, databases, and telecommunications, as well as grammar programs and a thesaurus.

Executive workstations are now a reality. Executives are performing clerical tasks, too, on their microcomputers.

- Laptop computers—A compact computer small enough to be placed on a lap and carried any place.
- Palmtop computers (also called personal digital assistants (PDAs)—Offers enhanced communications capabilities in either a pocket or handheld computer form.
- Optical character recognition—A reader that scans handwritten, printed, or typed information from paper and transfers it to a computer.
- Speakerphone—Frees users from holding the telephone receiver when conversing with others. For example, when the secretary has to check the files for specific information, he or she can communicate from any position in the office.

THE EXPANDING ROLE OF THE SECRETARY

The role of secretaries continues to grow mainly because they are in the right office technology environment at the right time. As the technology was introduced into the office, secretaries had to learn how to handle the equipment and software programs being used. They developed more sophisticated skills to process information. Then as downsizing was occurring, secretaries began assuming managerial responsibilities and emerged with more challenging jobs. A poll of members of the Professional Secretaries International reported that 94.7 percent of the respondents stated that their responsibilities increased in 1997. Some of the areas in which duties grew are the following:

Table 4. AREAS OF GROWTH

Administrative	70.3%
Computers/Technology	34.1%
Supervision	24.9%
Human Resources	18.9%

Source: "Nine Out of Ten Administrative Professionals Report Increased Responsibilities," Professional Secretaries International, 1997, http://www.psi.org/neews_9.html, 7/9/98.

The explosion of office technology has definitely changed the way in which many office tasks are performed, who does the work, and what kinds of work are done. Computers have been the major thrust for these changes and have evolved into global communication tools as well as an integral part of business.

New procedures for work flow and completion of tasks are created and constantly revised. Goals are set, productivity is logged in and out, production is measured, formats are standardized, and secretaries are accountable. The secretaries who work in an automated environment must understand the pattern of work flow so that they can understand relationships. Experts state that automation doesn't occur unless every person at every level, every thing, and every piece of equipment is integrated.

The phrase "just a secretary"—an individual who types correspondence and reports, who handles the telephone and clients, and who files and maintains a daily calendar—is a misnomer today. Secretaries are assuming more administrative responsibilities and are performing a variety of managerial functions, previously undertaken by lower-level managers. Secretaries now have an opportunity to be recognized for their special abilities and contributions to the management team.

Secretaries have an expanded role in the modern office as managers of information. Their responsibilities can run from scheduling staff appointments to office management to managing an entire database. In today's world of work, this is a profession that not only calls for the execution of a wide range of specialized tasks but is also combined with changes in business technology. As stated by Alan B. Bernstein, this "has led secretaries to turn to one another for support, training, and solidarity."[5]

Today's administrative professional, a designation for the wide field that includes secretaries, actually maintains a "multifaceted position that requires skills in organization, interpersonal communications, computer applications, negotiation, and time management."[6] The new role of the administrative professional focuses on three growth areas:

1. Computer software experts who play a central role in processing and distributing information. The findings of the 1997 study, "Benchmarking the Profession: PSI Membership Profile," reveals the extent to which administrative professionals use software. As expected, the greatest usage of computers is for word processing, which is 98.6 percent; 89.2 percent set up data into spreadsheets; 73.1 percent create presentation graphics; 58.2 percent input and retrieve information from databases; and 30.1 percent use desktop publishing software to create manuscripts and various types of literature. Most reflective of the new role of secretaries is the use of on-line services to conduct research, which is 53.2 percent.

2. Project managers who have been moving from short-term clerical tasks to multitask projects that involve greater responsibilities. A

Table 5. USAGE OF SOFTWARE BY ADMINISTRATIVE PROFESSIONALS

Word Processing	98.6%
Spreadsheets	89.2%
Presentation Graphics	73.1%
Database	58.2%
Desktop Publishing	30.1%
On-line Services	53.2%

---

[5]Alan B. Bernstein, "Secretary," *The Princeton Review,* New York: Random House, Inc., 1996, p. 352.

[6]"Benchmarking the Profession: PSI Membership Profile," Professional Secretaries, International, 1997.

large number of staff, 86.9 percent, now compose correspondence for both themselves and their managers.

3. Supervisors and trainers who also represent their departments at meetings.

If you are interested in a secretarial career, you must accept the fact that change is constant in automated offices and that all levels of personnel are affected. For example, more and more executives can be seen using the computer for inputting as well as for decision making. What you must realize is that computer systems are just tools for office personnel to use in performing their duties. Yes, you need to become computer literate to be able to operate equipment and use a variety of software packages; but more important are your knowledge of how computers work, your ability to analyze and solve a problem, your understanding of the ways in which new technology can be used, and your willingness to continue to learn and to adapt to changes.

HINTS FOR SUCCESS IN YOUR CAREER

The office workplace offers many more opportunities for a career with growth potential than ever before. It is up to you to make things happen. You must learn as much as you can about yourself, your needs, and your career goals—both short- and long-range.

You can gain insight about the secretarial career path by reading the literature. The consensus on the following comments is clearly indicated: secretaries are currently receiving greater respect than ever before; organizations are relying more on management skills of secretaries; secretaries are members of the management team; and more managerial duties are being delegated to secretaries. Below are some suggestions to open doors to upward mobility.

- Focus on the group's goals and objectives.
- Maintain a positive image.
- Use initiative, innovation, and creativity.
- Adopt a management frame of mind.
- Become cross-trained and learn as much as you can about your department.

- Make lifelong learning a goal through seminars, workshops, and college enrollment.
- Become a computer software expert.
- Be flexible and a good team player.
- Develop and focus on good interpersonal skills.
- Develop leadership qualities.
- Become a good organizer and know where and how to search for information needed to manage projects.

Secretaries say: "Well-trained secretaries who take their career seriously can reach for the stars." "Being a secretary is a dynamic career." "Practice being a 'people' person." Other qualities mentioned are the importance of a positive attitude, building a good rapport with the employer, polishing language skills, continuing one's education, adapting to change, and being willing to accept challenges.

CHAPTER 4

SECRETARIES ARE STILL IN DEMAND

Jobs that were once considered solid careers have now declined due to societal, global, and scientific forces that have led to the creation of new positions. According to the Bureau of Labor Statistics, total employment between now and 2006 will grow slower than it had in the past. This is because of changing methods in the way in which production and services are provided, such as changes in business technology and services. Most of the projected employment increase is in the services division, both business and health, of the service-production sector of the economy. An example of an employment decline in the field would be typists and word processors resulting from the growing use of word-processing equipment that increases efficiency and encourages office personnel to do more of the work themselves.

Secretarial and clerical work, referred to as "administrative support occupations, including clerical work" in the Department of Labor publications, will continue to employ the largest number of workers, even though employment will grow at a slower pace than average. This occurs because of the large number of employees required in the field and the high turnover rate. There should also be opportunities for full- and part-time work.

Although the explosion of office technology has been viewed by many as a threat to job security, the reverse is true. Office employment has been dramatically altered in number, type, responsibility, and nature of jobs available. The introduction of new services, as well as new products, has led to the creation of new kinds of jobs. Even though office automation increased productivity, it has been offset by secretaries assuming responsibilities that were previously in the domain of managers and other professionals. In addition to this, soft skills such as flexibility, a positive personality, a self-starter quality, use of discretion and diplomacy, and ability to be a team player are requirements employers want employees to possess.

If you wish to find work overseas, don't become overly optimistic because such jobs are not as plentiful or as attainable. The best approach to finding such a job is to become employed by the corporate headquarters of an international firm in the United States and then work toward this goal. You should also be aware that some countries place limitations on number and types of jobs that can be filled by foreigners and that the wages earned are frequently lower than comparable jobs in the United States.

EMPLOYMENT STATISTICS

In 1996, 3,403,000 secretaries and 1,369,000 clerical supervisors and managers were employed in the United States, according to the U.S. Department of Labor. Compared to the 1994 data, these figures represent a growth of 54,000 secretaries and 29,000 clerical supervisors and managers. In Canada, 400,000 administrative professionals/secretaries are employed.

Knowing what the future projections of a particular career field are is important so that you can make a wise decision. Individuals have certain preferences about environments in which they would like to work; therefore, examining job opportunities from an industry perspective is desirable. The data presented in the tables below will give you some comparison of the employment and percent change expected by 2006 in several types of industries.

Health Services. This is the largest industry in the country, with almost eleven million jobs. Employment in the health services sector is expected to increase more than twice as fast as the economy as a whole and add over three million jobs by 2006. Offices for physicians or dentists account for two-thirds of all private health service establishments. The bulk of the jobs in offices and clinics of physicians are in administrative support occupations, such as receptionist and medical secretaries, who consist of two-fifths of the workers in physicians' offices. However, hospitals employ the largest percentage of workers. As a secretary, you should become familiar with several health specialties to determine if any are of interest to you.

In Table 6, you will note that the employment number of secretaries for the industry is 181,000 and indicates a percentage of growth of 14.4 percent to 2006. Medical secretaries show that 235,000 secretaries are employed with a 32 percent growth rate expected between 1996–2006.

Management and Public Relation Services. Management services furnish administrative services, and management consulting offers operational advice. Public relations helps achieve favorable public exposure for clients and develops strategies for them to obtain a certain public image. The administrative support occupations together with the executive, administrative, and managerial occupations account for 53 percent of employment. Table 7 shows that in 1996, 48,000 secretaries were employed in this industry with a 33 percent change expected from 1996–2006.

Personnel supply services. This industry consists of employment agencies and help supply services. The help supply services companies provide temporary help to other businesses to supplement their workforce in special situations, such as during employee absences or increased seasonal workload. The help supply services firm contracts out to a "client"

Table 6. HEALTH SERVICES, 1996–2006

(Numbers in thousands)

Occupation	1996 Employment		1996–2006 Percent change
	Number	Percent	
Administrative support	1,995	19.0	27.7
General office clerks	316	3.0	55.0
Receptionists and information clerks	316	3.0	28.0
Medical secretaries	235	2.2	32.0
Secretaries, except legal and medical	181	1.7	14.4
Clerical supervisors and managers	144	1.4	39.8
Bookkeeping, accounting, and auditing clerks	117	1.1	13.5
Billing, cost, and rate clerks	112	1.1	36.0

Source: *Career Guide to Industries,* Bulletin 2503, January 1998.

Table 7. MANAGEMENT AND PUBLIC RELATIONS SERVICES, 1996–2006

(Numbers in thousands)

Occupation	1996 Employment		1996–2006 Percent change
	Number	Percent	
All occupations	873	100.0	60.3
Administrative support, including clerical	219	25.1	42.1
Secretaries	48	5.5	33.0
General office clerks	34	4.0	44.3
Bookkeeping, accounting, and auditing clerks	22	2.6	34.2
Clerical supervisors and managers	18	2.0	67.7
Receptionists and information clerks	15	1.7	67.7
Material recording, scheduling, dispatching, and distributing occupations	10	1.1	60.7
Typists, including word processing	9	1.1	9.0
Executive, administrative, and managerial	243	27.9	64.5
General managers and top executives	54	6.2	62.5
Financial managers	25	2.8	67.7
Marketing, advertising, and public relations managers	20	2.3	84.5
Administrative services managers	20	2.3	28.5
Management analysts	19	2.2	55.9
Accountants and auditors	16	1.8	55.3
Engineering, science, and computer systems managers	12	1.3	101.3

Source: *Career Guide to Industries,* Bulletin 2503, January 1998.

temporary workers at a specified fee. Many companies are especially receptive to hiring these temps even full-time rather than employing permanent staff who require significantly greater employee benefits. This industry encompasses a wide range of fields from administrative support occupations, such as secretary, to professional occupations, such as nurse. Secretaries are needed in every phase of business, including banks, insurance companies, investment and real estate firms, law firms, educational institutions, as well as in federal, state, and local government agencies. Obviously, employment will increase for all secretaries, including medical. Personnel supply services is one of the fastest-growing industries and one that is expected to provide the most new jobs, which are expected to grow 53 percent over the 1996–2006 period. This is almost four times the 14 percent growth anticipated for all industries combined. Table 8 shows that 192,000 secretaries were employed in 1996 with a 32.7 percent change from 1996–2006.

Table 8. PERSONNEL SUPPLY SERVICES, 1996–2006

(Numbers in thousands)

Occupation	1996 Employment		1996–2006 Percent change
	Number	Percent	
All occupations	2,646	100.0	52.7
Administrative support, including clerical	1,061	40.1	36.0
Secretaries	192	7.3	32.7
General office clerks	176	6.7	8.0
Typists, including word processing	131	5.0	8.8
Receptionists and information clerks	104	3.9	67.3
File clerks	76	2.9	43.4
Data entry keyers, except composing	70	2.6	33.9
Bookkeeping, accounting, and auditing clerks	48	1.8	33.9
Stock clerks	37	1.4	67.3

Source: *Career Guide to Industries,* Bulletin 2503, January 1998.

Social services. This industry usually appeals to individuals who are interested in helping others. The need exists in this industry, like in many others, for secretaries and other administrative support workers as well as managers. Generally, earnings of nonsupervisory personnel are below the average for all private industry. However, job opportunities should be excellent because of an expected 49 percent increase from 1996–2006, compared to only 14 percent for all industries. Table 9 shows 61,000 employed secretaries in 1996 with a growth rate of 21.3 percent.

SECRETARIAL/CLERICAL OCCUPATIONS IN CANADA

The fastest-growing sector in Canada's economy is the service sector, which is typical of the United States, thus accounting for the largest increase in jobs. Approximately two-thirds of all Canadians are employed in this category. The data and information that follow about clerical occupations, general office skills (includes administrative and office assistants); secretaries, recorders, and transcriptionists; medical

Table 9. SOCIAL SERVICES, 1996–2006

(Numbers in thousands)

Occupation	1996 Employment		1996–2006 Percent change
	Number	Percent	
Administrative support, including clerical	239	13.0	29.6
Secretaries	61	3.3	21.3
General office clerks	37	2.0	28.4
Bookkeeping, accounting, and auditing clerks	30	1.6	22.5
Receptionists and information clerks	27	1.5	52.6
Teacher aides and educational assistants	23	1.3	50.0
Executive, administrative, and managerial	219	11.9	50.6
General managers and top executives	80	4.3	50.7
Management support occupations	33	1.8	43.5
Financial managers	19	1.1	55.3

Source: *Career Guide to Industries,* Bulletin 2503, January 1998.

secretaries; and legal secretaries present an overview of the field. Secretarial work is a predominantly female occupation. See Table 10 for a comparison of employment statistics between 1984–1994.

Clerical occupations, general office skills, employees work primarily for government and the private sector. Fifty-two percent are general office clerks and 32 percent are receptionists. Of this total, 21 percent work part-time, which is slightly more than the average for all occupations. Women account for 76 percent of the clerical workers. Employment is moderately sensitive to business conditions, and the technological change does have a negative effect on the group due to computers, facsimile equipment, electronic mail, and related software. The largest number of clerical staff work in finance, insurance, and real estate followed by 78 percent for the federal administration.

Secretaries, recorders, and transcriptionists work in government and throughout the private sector including law offices, real estate companies, hospitals and doctors' offices, and other types of organizations. This group includes specialized secretaries such as technical, medical, legal, estate, and litigation secretaries as well as court reporters and stenographers.

Of this group, 421,000 were employed in 1994, which is 3 percent of the workforce. Secretaries account for 80 percent of the group, and women make up 92 percent of all these workers.

Medical secretaries work in doctors' offices, hospitals, clinics, and other medical settings. Of this group, 51.4 percent work in physicians, health practitioners and medical labs, followed by 35.9 percent who work in

Table 10. SECRETARIAL/CLERICAL EMPLOYMENT IN CANADA, 1994

Title	1994	1984–1994
	Employment Number	Percent Change
Clerical Occupations, General Office Skills	356,000	11
Secretaries, Recorders, and Transcriptionists	421,000	3
Medical Secretaries	37,000	18
Legal Secretaries	37,000	3

Source: *Job Futures,* Vol. 1: Occupational Outlook, 1995.

hospitals. In 1994, 37,000 were employed as medical secretaries, a growth of 18 percent more than 1984. Twenty-four percent of the medical secretaries work part-time, well above the average for all occupations. In this specialty, 99 percent are women. It is interesting to note that private health care practices continue to be the center for job creation in this occupation.

Legal secretaries work in government, law offices, land title offices, and in courts at the municipal, provincial, and federal levels. In this group, the large majority work in professional offices—81 percent. The number of legal secretaries employed in this profession in 1994 was 37,000, a growth rate of 3 percent more than in 1984. When compared to medical secretaries, a substantial difference in growth rate between 1984 and 1994 exists (15 percent). Part-timers account for 11 percent of the employees. In this specialty, too, 99 percent are women. It should be noted that most of the employment growth for legal secretaries is projected to be in private law practices. See Table 10 to note employment figures that range from 37,000 each for medical and legal secretarial employees to 421,000 for secretaries, recorders, and transcriptionists. The percent of growth of employment economywide is 17 percent.

LABOR FORCE PARTICIPATION RATES OF WOMEN AND MEN

Labor force participation rates of men and women are changing. Women will continue to have a huge stake in the current and future labor force, although at a slower rate than previously. The overall participation rate for women is expected to rise by about 2 percent, half of what it was the previous decade. This increase will be among the forty-five to sixty-four year old women who will replace the younger women. By 2006, the women's share of the labor force will be 47.4 percent. In effect, women's participation rates will increase for all age groups over nineteen, except for the group aged sixty-five and over. The participation rates for working men will decline below age forty-five, except for those aged sixteen to nineteen years, which will remain steady at 53 percent. The rate for age group forty-five and above will increase. Table 11 shows the continual rise of women in the labor force and the slow

Table 11. PERCENTAGE OF MEN'S AND WOMEN'S
PARTICIPATION IN THE LABOR FORCE, 1976–2006

Source: *Occupational Outlook Quarterly,* winter 1997–98, p. 28.

decline for men, although men still lead. The men's participation rates in the labor forces at all ages is higher than those for women.

MALE-FEMALE EMPLOYMENT IN SECRETARIAL WORK

The secretarial field is one of the largest. The 1998 statistics showed that 3,616,000 of men and women aged sixteen and over were employed in secretarial work. The number of men in that age range was 81,000 and women, 3,535,000. For the twenty-year-and-over group for the same period, 76,000 men were employed and 3,412,000 women.

With the changes that are occurring, there appears to be a blurring of the traditional demarcation between jobs for men and women. Is this a reality in secretarial employment, a predominately female-intensive occupation? Although we cannot respond positively that the numbers of men have increased substantially in this field, we can state that more men are enrolling in office administration curricula. This might be the result of variations in department names to reflect the nature of the field and changing responsibilities of secretarial personnel. Some new titles are: department of office technology, office and systems administration, and department of secretarial and office information systems. Men are gradually becoming attracted to this career because of the changing work environment and the diverse opportunities that exist. Many men who are secretaries work with dynamic business and professional people, often within the medical, legal, entertainment, and publishing environments.

Some comments from men who were secretaries revealed the following reasons for pursuing this field: "Serving others and being at the top of things and networking with counterparts are only a few of the rewards achieved from this career." "Successful secretaries have adapted to the Information Age by expanding their job skills. They realized long ago that knowledge is power." "The profession was intriguing since very few males sought entrance, and I wanted to secure a future with skills that would be helpful in landing a job." Other reasons for men entering the field include nationwide opportunities in a variety of industries and the challenge of involvement with high technology and challenging responsibilities.

THE ALTERNATIVE WORKPLACE

The traditional office environment is no longer the sole focus of the workplace. Alternative workplaces that incorporate nontraditional locations and practices are being supplemented. This is a transformation that moves the work to the worker. What precipitated this movement? Women account for a large percentage of the labor force. They are now interested in lifelong careers and frequently are multiple jobholders. What do these changes in lifestyles, values, and social patterns mean in terms of employment? First, firms want to retain their valuable employees. Women need to balance their work and home life; therefore, it is necessary to adopt innovative work patterns that are flexible in work schedules and locations. Second, since women have the needed skills and productive capacity to help support the country's economic growth, business has to respond to their needs by establishing alternative work patterns that would spur recruitment, improve morale, and reduce absenteeism and turnover. Another important reason for developing alternative work patterns is to reduce the amount of space utilized and lower overhead costs. AT&T, as stated in the *Harvard Business Review* of

May/June 1998, indicated that by eliminating offices people don't need, consolidating others, and reducing related overhead costs, they freed up $550 million in cash flow. At IBM, a survey of employees in their Mobility Initiative plan " revealed that 87 percent believe that their personal productivity and effectiveness on the job have increased significantly." AmEx's alternative plan "helps the company retain experienced employees who find the flexibility to work from home especially attractive."[1] This section will explore how and where work can be done and the many forms an alternative workplace can take.

Part-Time Work

Part-time workers are the largest group of employees performing less than full-time responsibilities. Generally, these workers are students, young people not ready for full-time commitments, mothers who need the extra income but only want to work while their young children are in school, or mature individuals with family responsibilities. Part-time employment means working less than thirty-five hours a week; however, the usual time frame is to work three days a week or twenty hours per week.

Today part-time employment is used in different ways, according to the Department of Labor. Individuals combine several part-time jobs to make up a full workweek. Another pattern is to hold a full-time primary job and a part-time secondary job. Approximately eight million workers held more than one job at a time, and more than half of all moonlighters in 1997 combined a full-time job with a part-time job, according to the February 1998 Monthly Labor Review. In the administrative support profession, approximately 6.5 percent of total employment were multiple jobholders

Opportunities for employment in secretarial positions as part-timers continue to increase, for employers see the benefits in reduced labor costs and flexibility in hiring staff when needed. Kelly Services of Troy, Michigan, and Manpower Inc., of Milwaukee, Wisconsin, two of the largest sources of part-timers, report that the need for part-timers has grown so fast that they cannot readily fill temporary job openings.

---

[1]Mahlon Apgar, IV, "The Alternative Workplace: Changing Where and How People Work," *Harvard Business Review* (May/June 1998): 121–22.

Compressed Workweek

In some businesses, a scheduling alternative is available. Instead of working a full five-day week schedule, a popular option is to compress the forty hours into a four-day week. Another choice is to work twelve hours a day for three days. This type of scheduling allows for extended hours for the company and a weekday for employees to use for personal responsibilities.

TEMPORARY EMPLOYMENT

The traditional idea of hiring a temporary employee to fill in for a receptionist who is sick or on vacation has changed radically in the past few years. Temporary help performing all sorts of work is used throughout the company. This type of hiring falls into the category of contract staffing in which the temporary employee is obtained from a help supply service firm that is the employer of this individual. Much of this started with global competition and downsizing. Advantages for the company for which the temp works are the following: available staff without the burden of paying for benefits, fewer layoffs in slow seasons, decrease in record keeping, replacement of unsatisfactory workers, and screening of employees for qualifications and experience. The data reflect that the use of temps has increased 240 percent in the last decade and will probably continue to grow. The benefits for the temporary worker are experience in different types of organizations, development of skills, and growing list of references.

Two other trends in staffing the office are *outsourcing* and *employee leasing.* Outsourcing is a form of contract staffing that transfers business functions to a third party. Smaller companies frequently use outsourcing because they can't justify a full-time experienced employee on staff, or perhaps they have difficulty hiring and retaining such experts. Outsourcing may also be used to augment the manpower already on the payroll. Some midsize organizations are resorting to selective outsourcing where they off-load only one or two tasks. According to Chris Miksanek in the August 1997 issue of *Datamation,* "…87 percent of senior management is currently considering outsourcing."

In leasing, a long-term permanent arrangement, the customer has a contractual agreement with the leasing firm, which is the employer. The advantage of these two trends is that the customer never handles payroll, taxes, insurance benefits, vacations, or other administrative items.

If you are looking for challenge and excitement and want to become acquainted with different kinds of companies, temporary employment might be an approach you should investigate. Each day is different, for you never know what you are getting into. One basic advantage of working as a temp is the opportunity of determining whether you like the job and environment. This might also lead to a permanent job if you have the right skills and attitude. While you are working as a temp, take advantage of the training most temporary staffing agencies offer to make you more marketable.

Flextime

Flextime, a concept in scheduling daily work hours for full-time employees, is receiving favorable acceptance in many companies and continues to be adopted throughout the country. There are variations of flextime scheduling; however, personnel usually work during a core period each day. From options established by management, workers select the time that completes a day's productivity. For example, employees might have the choice of arriving at work between 6:30 A.M. and 10:00 A.M. and leaving between 3:00 P.M. and 6:30 P.M. Thus, employees have some control over their workday. Occasionally, a company will offer a four-day workweek that narrows down to a ten-hour day.

Flextime has resulted in positive effects on employee attitudes, and sick leave is less abused. A recent business survey indicated that more firms are adopting flextime scheduling. They claim it increases efficiency and morale and decreases absenteeism and turnover. One can assume from this finding that as personnel satisfaction increases, company image is improved. This gives a firm a competitive advantage in the marketplace. Productivity usually is maintained or increased, and many employee benefits are realized. Although flextime was originally designed for lower-level employees, some Fortune 500 organizations are now extending this work pattern to managers and professional employees.

Telecommuting

Telecommuting is one of the most recognized forms of alternative workplaces. Work is performed electronically wherever the employee is and frequently supplements the traditional office rather than replacing it.

Telecommuting, also referred to as the electronic cottage, initially involved people working at home or at a satellite office on a computer or terminal and communicating by phone to the home office. This concept has been broadened and includes those individuals who work out of a customer's office or who communicate with the office via laptop or mobile telephone. Interestingly, Alvin Toffler in 1980 in his book *The Third Wave* predicted that millions of Americans would establish automated work centers in their homes. His predictions became a reality as computers, fax machines, and modems became accessible in terms of pricing, and America grew into an information-based society.

Is the office becoming obsolete? Although we may never witness its complete extinction, there is every reason to believe that there will be a substantial reduction in the physical office. Increasing numbers of employees work at home.

Companies vary widely in the approaches they use with home offices. Some allow employees to use their own discretion. Others, such as AT&T, IBM, and Lucent Technologies, provide laptops, dedicated phone lines, software support, fax-printer units, help lines, and full technical backup at the nearest corporate facility.[2]

One health-related facility implemented a telecommuting program because it became increasingly difficult to find qualified medical secretaries. Management worked out a program whereby physicians dictated over the telephone to a central system, secretaries accessed the information through telephone lines, and the documents were transcribed on computers. At a scheduled time each evening, the day's work was transmitted back on communication lines to the clinic where it was printed.

Of course, there are many concerns about whether telecommuting will really work in the long run because employees cannot develop a sense of belonging that fulfills psychological needs, nor can they be part of the informal interaction in the office. Another disadvantage is the

---

[2]Ibid., 124.

inability to be a team player because a home-based work environment doesn't permit the employee to have that kind of interactive work experience. Also, communication via e-mail is not a substitute for personal interaction.

If you plan to be a telecommuting worker, follow the tips for success outlined below:

- Plan your working hours without interruptions.
- Design an organized working environment.
- Maintain a work agenda for you and your manager to review.
- Plan regular meetings at the office with your supervisor or manager.
- Become part of a team or group and attend regular meetings at the office.
- Communicate by e-mail or in writing of progress of work at the beginning of each week.
- Keep your workplace at home private.
- Share your home office with your coworkers for meetings.
- Network with other telecommuters and staff.

Job Sharing

Another alternative to full-time employment is job sharing where two people assume responsibilities for a job. They divide the work between them and arrange their own schedules to provide full-time coverage on the job. Job sharing differs from part-time work in which an individual is an independent employee who has the sole responsibility for a particular job.

Advocates of nontraditional work groups point out several advantages of job sharing:

- Job sharers are interested in careers and advancement.
- Productivity will probably increase because of greater job satisfaction, more concentrated effort, and lower rate of absenteeism and turnover.
- Coverage can be arranged during peak periods or absenteeism due to sickness.
- Greater continuity occurs in job performance. If one of the job sharers leaves the job, the partner can usually fill in while a new person is being trained.

Unless carefully planned, job sharing can be a failure, too. Some factors companies consider are recognition of each individual's strengths and weaknesses, parity with full-time positions in terms of salaries and benefits, clearly understood expectations, and voluntary job sharing. Personnel factors to be taken into account when establishing such a working arrangement are good communication skills, organizational ability, cooperativeness, and similarity of work values.

Although many employers have expressed resistance to such programs, others endorse the concept and have initiated it.

CHAPTER 5

PERCEPTIONS OF SECRETARIES

Technology, downsizing, and our global business world have combined to eliminate the old methods of working and to present many challenges to the secretary that will continue into the next millenium. Fewer and fewer secretaries function in traditional roles as Gals Friday. Position descriptors of secretaries differ depending on the specific responsibilities of the job. In the past, the categorization of secretaries was always office support personnel, but today even that varies. It is not uncommon to see category designations as "office professionals," "office administrators," or "administrative support/clerical." When word processing first developed, the secretarial role was restructured into two distinct types of functions: typing and nontyping. The nontyping role was handled by the administrative secretary who supported principals, executives, and managers in contrast to the typing or correspondence secretary who worked in document production environments. Career paths for upward mobility existed along these lines.

Secretaries are employed in every type of industry, profession, and institution: insurance, banks and financial firms, law, medical and health care organizations, education, airlines, travel agencies, philanthropic and religious groups, manufacturing, real estate, advertising, publishing, radio and television, public utilities, and personnel supply services. However, today, the office is not necessarily within the confines of the organization but can be almost anywhere and anyplace—at home, in a restaurant, in an airline terminal, or in a hotel.

Secretarial jobs vary depending on the type of firm, size of company, specialization, and philosophy of the company. In large firms, secretaries are assigned to a particular department, and companywide procedures are established for handling certain administrative tasks. In smaller offices, secretaries undoubtedly handle diverse responsibilities and are able to exercise more independence in carrying out specific tasks. They also receive a broad range of experiences.

No matter whether it is a multinational firm or small business, secretarial work evolves around new office automation and company restructuring. New strategies based on controlling costs and improving productivity are changing the way business is done, which affects secretarial workers. Generally, their roles and responsibilities have expanded. The workload of secretaries is increasing, tasks are more varied, and they are assuming management duties and obligations. Secretaries basically manage information. Their responsibilities run the gamut from producing correspondence and reports to scheduling staff appointments to office management to managing an entire database. Few professions require such skillful knowledge and ability to execute so many specialized tasks. A 1994 study by the Administrative Development Institute that included 174 U.S. and Canadian members of the Professional Secretaries International found that secretaries were given more managerial duties after downsizing decimated the middle management level. Some management duties are maintaining and purchasing equipment and supplies and hiring, training, and supervising personnel.[1] In the same study, McEwen received very good feedback on feelings of secretaries about their new role and duties. Most of the 71 percent of the secretaries who had been assigned managerial duties had positive feelings about their careers; 68 percent stated this gave them opportunities for professional growth; 51 percent indicated they received more respect; and 51 percent believed the new responsibilities brought them into the management teams.

Administrative support personnel need to have a broad set of skills that include document processing, distribution of information, managing records and files, organizing and planning, maintaining equipment and supplies, and performing financial functions. Increasingly, secretaries are producing spreadsheets and databases as well as using desktop publishing and graphics programs. Clearly these qualifications show the

---

[1]Beryl C. McEwen, "Preparing Office Professionals for the Next Century," *Business Education Forum* (October 1997): 42.

need to be computer literate and technology oriented to be successful. Secretaries must learn to think like managers. With this change comes more empowerment and freedom in their jobs as well as responsibility.

Those secretaries who do highly specialized work, such as in the legal and medical fields, need to understand the terminology and procedures used in these environments. More information is given later in this chapter.

Chapter 3 referred to the variety of titles for secretaries that are being used today. Added to that list can be specialized secretary, senior secretary/assistant, transcription specialist, administrative receptionist, and word processing/administrative assistant. These designations frequently don't reflect the qualifications, duties, and responsibilities of the secretarial positions. As mentioned previously, few other professionals have to be capable of performing such a variety of tasks and projects. Jobs vary and require different skills for the nature of the position. When searching for a job, look under the various titles. Read the ads very carefully and be prepared to ask questions about the job to determine if it will be a good experience with potential for you.

There is a constant need for secretaries in many industries, whether it be in traditional business offices, automated environments, or offices of specialists. The field is one of the largest; therefore, new recruits always will be required. Also, many secretarial duties are of an interactive nature and not easily automated. For example, planning conferences, working with clients, and dealing with staff require tact and diplomacy as well as communication skills. Automated equipment cannot substitute for these personal skills; therefore, secretaries will continue to play an important role in most organizations. In addition to the general, behavioral, and technical secretarial skills, employers may seek individuals who have specialized training or experience in technical, legal, or medical areas.

This chapter will introduce you to the many professional secretarial career specializations to help you choose the career best suited to your own interests and talents.

THE IMAGE OF SECRETARIAL PERSONNEL

In the traditional office, secretaries generally work on a one-to-one relationship with the principal. However, that is atypical today; secretaries usually are assigned to several individuals. It is the senior partner who may still be supported by the traditional secretary, who functions as a generalist, performs diverse tasks, uses a computer for document production, and is knowledgeable about office routines and procedures as well as the organization. Responsibilities of the general secretary, no matter what the title is, might include duties extending into personnel administration, supervision, management, and other areas.

The National Compensation Survey has replaced the *White-Collar Pay: Private Goods-Producing Industries,* published by the U.S. Department of Labor. Ten criteria are used to determine the levels or ranking of an occupation based on the requirements of the position. These factors are taken from the U.S. Government Office of Personnel Management's Factor Evaluation System:

1. Knowledge (tasks, rules, operations, tools, equipment, etc.)
2. Supervision received (e.g., extent of direct and indirect controls exercised by supervisor and setting of priorities and deadlines)
3. Guidelines (e.g., judgment needed to apply procedures and policies; use of reference manuals)
4. Complexity (number, variety, and intricacy of tasks and methods in work performed)
5. Scope and effect (depth of assignment and effect on others)
6. Personal contact (ability to communicate)
7. Purpose of contacts (kinds of exchanges such as giving facts or resolving problems)
8. Physical demands (demands work assignment places on employee)
9. Work environment (considers risks and discomforts of surroundings)
10. Supervisory duties (describes level of supervisory responsibility)

The Bureau of Labor Statistics develops data on five levels of secretaries. Level 1 is the entry level where an employee performs duties under specific instructions of a supervisor and handles a general range of office duties including inputting on a computer, transcribing dictation, and performing other office functions. On level 2, the secretary works under the supervisor's general instructions, and on level 3 exercises judgment and initiative to take in nonroutine situations and works with the approval of the supervisor on other situations. By level 4, the employee is handling independently a wide variety of situations and conflicts involving clerical or administrative functions of the office.

Level 5 is the highest level of achievement and has a significant number of managerial responsibilities.

The long-standing definition of secretary adopted by the Professional Secretaries International depicts this employee as a highly qualified person who possesses not only a mastery of office skills but also personal requisites of the highest order. A secretary is "an executive assistant who possesses a mastery of office skills, demonstrates the ability to assume responsibility without direct supervision, exercises initiative and judgment, and makes decisions within the scope of assigned authority." To be more inclusive and because many businesses are changing the title of secretary to reflect the scope of the evolving responsibilities of the position, an addition had been added to the name of the organization: Professional Secretaries International: The Association for Office Professionals. As of August 1, 1998, the name is International Association of Administrative Professionals.

Secretaries in traditional offices are generalists or individuals who perform all support functions. Secretaries are basically information workers who process and transmit information within and outside the organization. They must possess certain intangible qualities that are not easily measured to carry out the duties of the position. For example, the secretary must be able to make value judgments as to the importance of incoming communications and telephone calls, items that require immediate responses, communications that can be answered by the secretary, calls that can be transferred to another staff member, and documents that should be held for future reference.

Another important aspect of the secretarial position is the interaction with executives, managers, staff, clients, and suppliers. Are good human relations skills being used? Is the secretary presenting a favorable image of the office and company?

Word Processing

The development of word processors led to a more complex automated environment than the traditional office. Large corporations began to establish *centralized work areas* where word processing specialists handled work from the company at large. When completed, the documents were returned to the principal or originator for signature before distribution. *Decentralized arrangements,* also referred to as *satellite stations* and *minicenters,* were established to support either a department, a specific division, or selected principals. Centralized work areas are still in operation in large firms; however, the nature of the work has changed to a large extent. Since the current trend is to have a computer on every desk, many employees input their own work. The centralized areas generally produce large projects: charts, graphics, and illustrations for presentations and distribution, and specialized tasks.

As the competition began to force prices down, small firms started to purchase electronic typewriters with automated word processing features and microcomputers with a diversity of software programs for document processing, statistical worksheets, and database management. This equipment was placed on the desks of secretaries and led to the transformation of the secretaries and other members of the office staff into *end users,* particularly for word processing. Currently, secretaries and other office staff use computers primarily for word processing applications.

Manufacturers do agree, however, that a firm must install a system that matches its needs. Logically, large corporations will focus on systems that interact and include some of the following PC-based office applications: word processing, electronic mail, centralized storage and electronic filing cabinets, spreadsheets, database, graphics, data processing, voice processing, image processing, telecommunications, and teleconferencing. Smaller firms do not require the same degree of sophisticated systems. Ultimately, each firm, from small to large, aims to increase the productivity of all office workers, including executives, managers, and secretaries.

There is great diversity in capabilities of computers with word processing software applications. In addition to creating documents quickly, secretaries can perform many other functions very easily: rearranging text without rekeying; producing complex documents with graphics and tables; merging information from several sources to produce one document; automatic pagination; global search (replacing one word throughout the text with another); justification; incorporating lines, boxes, and logos within a document; and inserting headers and footers. In the merging operation, you can store separately a list of names and addresses, a form letter and selected paragraphs. Information can be retrieved from all three sources to produce personalized letters or general form letters to be distributed throughout the country.

Communicating word processors can also send a communication to an office in a distant city, thus bypassing the postal service. It is also possible to integrate a table, for example, from one software program to another. Other word processing features are the spell check, thesaurus for finding synonyms and antonyms for selected words, and grammar and style programs to help in writing tasks.

This automated equipment together with the sophisticated systems that have been evolving have created dramatic changes in the office environment with resulting effects on secretarial staff. Office automation has opened up many exciting, challenging job opportunities with career paths. This chapter will describe the diversity of positions available in automated environments. This will give you a better insight into the demands of the profession.

POSITION DESCRIPTIONS FOR GENERAL SECRETARIAL, ADMINISTRATIVE ASSISTANT, AND WORD PROCESSING PERSONNEL

As you read the job descriptions below, you will note that secretarial and administrative assistant are titles used interchangeably for the same type of position. Reference has been made to these variations in Chapter 3. However, there are differences between the word processing and the secretarial specializations. Word processing support staff handle the keyboarding tasks and document production for principals and other staff who either forward handwritten material or dictate directly to the centralized or decentralized center where the tapes are transcribed. Secretaries and administrative assistants perform a wide range of duties such as screening calls, receiving and directing visitors, filing, scheduling meetings, editing, gathering information, and keeping digests of mail.

The job descriptions that follow are used in the *1998 Salary Guide* of Office Team, a specialized administrative staffing service. Note the preference of this firm is to use the title "administrative assistant" before "secretary."

- Administrative Assistant/Secretary I (up to three years of experience) Performs administrative and office support activities for multiple supervisors; includes departmental secretaries. Duties may include fielding telephone calls, receiving and directing visitors, typing, word processing, filing, and faxing. Requires basic and intermediate computer expertise and strong communication skills.

- Administrative Assistant/Secretary II (three-plus years of experience)
  Duties include those described by Administrative Assistant/ Secretary I; support senior-level managers; maintain high-level of computer expertise with ability to train others in systems usage.
- Executive Assistant/Executive Secretary I (up to four years of experience)
  Performs administrative duties for senior management. Responsibilities may include screening calls, making travel and meeting arrangements, preparing reports and financial data, handling customer relations, and training and supervising other support staff. Requires intermediate-level computer skills, including proficiency with spreadsheet, presentation and database applications; flexibility; excellent interpersonal and communication skills; project coordinator expertise; and the ability to interact with all levels of management.
- Executive Assistant/Executive Secretary II (five-plus years of experience)
  Duties include those described for Executive Secretary I, advanced communication skills, ability to train others on systems usage; able to support the most senior management personnel, particularly in large corporations; and possibly supervise other administrative staff.
- Receptionist/Administrative Assistant
  Receives and routes telephone calls, greets visitors, handles filing, distributes mail, photocopies, faxes, provides administrative support at various levels within organization, and uses computer.

In the last chapter of this career guidance book, you will become familiar with the steps you will have to take in your job search. You may use the Internet to search for a job and submit your resume for a position on-line. Below are a few on-line ads that were entered by different companies.

- Office Manager
  Coordinates various office support services, including purchasing and facilities management. May include supervision of office administrative staff.

- Word Processor
  Creates, edits, and proofs a variety of documents; transcribes tapes; knows latest word processing software.
- Executive Word Processor
  Uses word progressing programs with emphasis on advanced projects; adapts to unfamiliar systems with minimal review; performs specialized functions such as graphics creations, troubleshooting, and integration of data from different software applications.

SPECIALIZED SECRETARIAL FIELDS

Four secretarial positions require specialized knowledge and abilities: legal, medical, technical, and educational.

Legal

The employment outlook for the legal secretary looks good. According to Gini Myers, Certified Professional Legal Secretary (PLS) and former National Association of Legal Secretaries (NALS) president, there is a shortage of qualified legal secretaries who have the knowledge necessary to work in a legal environment. (See Table 12 for distribution of employment by secretarial specialty.)

The role of the legal secretary has changed similar to that of the general secretary. Legal secretaries need to be computer literate,

Table 12. EMPLOYMENT BY SECRETARIAL SPECIALTY, 1996–2006

Title	Projected Employment		Employment % Change
	1996	2006	
Secretaries, total	3,403,000	3,427,000	1
Legal Secretaries	284,000	319,000	13
Medical Secretaries	239,000	314,000	32
Secretaries, except Legal and Medical	2,881,000	2,794,000	−3

Source: U.S. Department of Labor

understand the terminology, and have the specialized knowledge required in a legal environment. In the past, shorthand skills were a requirement; today is is looked upon very favorably in the higher-level positions and frequently is requested by senior partners. In some firms, legal secretaries conduct the research, schedule depositions, and answer clients' questions.

Legal secretaries prepare legal documents such as summonses, complaints, motions, petitions, subpoenas, answers, living trusts, deeds, affidavits, and briefs. They may also be in charge of the law library, adding parts and other material to update editions as the law and precedent change. In addition to the typical responsibilities of taking and transcribing dictation and performing administrative office functions required in any office, other duties include the following: reviewing law journals, assisting with legal research, taking notes on proceedings, maintaining corporate records, filing papers in the courthouse, taking notes, and maintaining lawyer's papers in order during trial; investigating cases for trial and obtaining information that the lawyer must have to prepare certain documents; advising lawyer of court appearances and due dates for filing pleadings; and maintaining escrow accounts.

Carol Ann Wilson, a certified legal secretary and member of the Certifying Board of the Legal Secretaries International, believes that the legal secretary, in addition to having office skills and personal traits that are far above average, should be an expert at time management, juggling many activities and roles at the same time; must possess psychological skills, dealing daily with many personalities; and must use excellent judgment to make dozens of critical decisions.

Several factors in the legal services field will impact the future of the legal secretary: 1. Clients want more accountability for fees they pay. 2. Paralegal firms exist that offer discounted rates for legal services, such as preparing wills, uncontested divorces, and name changes. These individuals are not lawyers and will affect the industry.

No two jobs in the legal profession are alike, with marked differences between the duties of a legal secretary in a one- or two-lawyer office compared to a large firm employing many lawyers. A special code of conduct is required of legal secretaries, which is spelled out in the Code of Ethics developed by the National Association of Legal Secretaries (International). Every member shall:

- Encourage respect for the law and the administration of justice.
- Observe the rules governing privileged communications and confidential information.
- Promote and exemplify high standards of loyalty, cooperation, and courtesy.
- Perform all duties of the profession with integrity and competence.
- Pursue a high order of professional attainment.

Being a legal secretary is one of the most highly respected positions in the secretarial field. Excellent office skills are necessary and the qualities that enable you to work well with highly trained professionals are desirable as well.

Job opportunities are unlimited for legal secretaries, with choices of specialization in patent, criminal, real estate, malpractice, corporation, matrimonial, probate, or negligence law. In recent years, environmental law and public interest law have also emerged. There is a trend toward increasing specialization in large law firms that employ large numbers of legal secretaries.

If you are interested in diverse activities, the small, private law firm might be for you. It offers the widest variety of work and the greatest opportunity for individual initiative. Large law firms or legal departments of corporations usually provide well-defined work. An advantage of corporate departments, however, is that hours of employment are more regular; in law firms, no matter what size, frequently the legal secretary is called upon to work overtime.

VIEWS FROM A SECRETARY AND LAWYER

Carol Ann Wilson stated: "I am very proud to be a legal secretary. I am proud of the knowledge and experience I have gained...I have met famous people, worked on important cases, been given important responsibilities, and learned more than I could from any law school. I have been trusted with information that is so confidential that, had I been working for the government, I would have had the highest security clearance...."

Luther J. Avery of Bancroft, Avery and McAlister in San Francisco, California, believes there is a need for qualified legal secretaries who perform a vital role in the delivery of legal services:

The legal profession and the delivery of legal services is involved in massive changes that reflect the changes occurring in society. Along with the changes affecting the law business, there are many changes in how legal services will be delivered.

Despite the changes, certain characteristics of law practice continue; notably, the personal and confidential relationship between lawyer and client; the intellectual stimulation from problem solving and helping people; and the need for quality services and attention to detail.

There is more need than ever for competent legal secretaries today; there is a shortage. There will be a need for competent legal secretaries in the future; and, I predict, a shortage.

The legal secretary may need more skills or more education, but that is part of the challenge that makes the job interesting. The competent legal secretary is and will continue to be an administrator, a facilitator, the key person on the law office production line who will help maintain the quality of legal products and services.

The essential skills, knowledge, and attitudes of the legal secretary are spelled out in the literature of such organizations as the National Association of Legal Secretaries. Where the lawyer-client relationship is dependent upon the integrity and intelligence of the participants and is responsive to personal problems, there is a continuing need for the professionalism that is exhibited by legal secretaries such as those who qualify as a Professional Legal Secretary and those who have the same skills, knowledge, and attitudes.

Without legal secretaries involved in the delivery of legal services, lawyers and the legal system would have difficulty functioning. If you are interested in employment as a legal secretary, try to obtain a broad education and learn management skills and computer skills as well as the skills of personnel relations, human relations, and skills as a technician. Most of all, in seeking employment as a legal secretary, be careful to select your employer wisely because whether or not you will enjoy the legal secretarial profession will probably depend upon the environment in which you function.

Medical

Professional specialty and service occupations in the health services industry cover nearly three out of five jobs, according to the Department of Labor statistics. The next largest share of jobs is in administrative support occupations.

The health-care industry has experienced unprecedented growth. The proliferation of medical centers, family practice clinics, extended health care facilities, private group practices, and long-term care facilities has created a need for secretaries with good office skills, a knowledge of medical terminology, training in administrative and clinical procedures, and a "caring" attitude.

Secretarial jobs and responsibilities in medical offices vary. For example, you might be responsible for business activities in the office, you might be the receptionist who greets patients when they walk into a doctor's office or hospital, or you might be an assistant who helps patients in preparing for examinations or for certain medical procedures such as taking blood pressure and temperature. As a medical secretary, you will have many opportunities for challenges of this nature.

Whether you choose to work in a small doctor's office or in a large medical center, you will undoubtedly perform diverse duties each day. In addition to handling the general office routines, you may prepare papers for hospital admissions, obtain patient information, maintain the appointment book, prepare information for referrals, complete insurance forms, arrange for payment of fees, keep reminders for renewals of licenses and memberships in organizations, order supplies and drugs, transcribe and maintain records of the patients' medical histories, and deal with pharmaceutical representatives who visit the office to discuss new products with the doctor.

As you become more familiar with the medical secretarial career, you will realize that in addition to hospitals, clinics, and private doctors' offices, you could find employment with a medical research foundation, in companies that manufacture drugs, in health-related organizations such as Blue Cross/Blue Shield, and in medical departments of large corporations that provide employees with health services.

In addition to promotional opportunities as a supervisor or manager, you may wish to become a medical assistant. In this position, you would continue to perform the typical secretarial and administrative tasks and would also perform clinical duties and procedures. The employment outlook for both types of medical secretarial careers is excellent. The Bureau of Labor Statistics predicts a 32 percent increase in employment from 1996 to the year 2006 for medical secretaries.

Have you ever thought of becoming a medical transcriptionist, another allied health career? Medical transcriptionists work with physicians, pharmacists, radiologists, nurses, and dieticians. A medical transcriptionist must know the language of medical and surgical specialties. They transcribe medical histories and physicals, operative reports, consultations, discharge summaries, and a long list of other subspecialty documentations. They need a command of medical terminology, very good keyboarding and editing skills, excellent auditory skills, and highly developed analytical skills. An individual who is interested in a career as a medical transcriptionist is assured of flexible work schedules and an intellectually challenging position.

A MEDICAL SECRETARY'S POINT OF VIEW

Janice Nicosia, an administrative assistant for a cardiologist at Massachusetts General Hospital in Boston, functions in a private setting on a one-to-one basis with the physician for whom she works. From her perspective as an employee in a hospital environment, she believes it is a very good, interesting, and rewarding field in which to be employed.

The medical field is changing in the way medical services are delivered and the type of insurance coverage for patients. Every secretary's role differs, based on whether you work in a hospital, private setting, or in a clinic in a hospital. In my position I handle practically everything for my boss. Some of my responsibilities are the following:

- Handle patient care by making appointments for the patients, which include their admissions for cardiac catherization and surgery; also coordinate other appointments such as tests that include exercise or vascular studies and neurology, depending on circumstances at the time.
- Transcribe 75 percent of the recorded dictation for my boss. Since the load of documents is excessive and it must be completed expeditiously, approximately 25 percent of it is sent to a transcription service.
- An aide does the xeroxing and filing, which is still traditional in setup.
- Access from the computer test results on patient's chest.
- Prepare preliminary report of tests taken, such as a stress test, a few hours after it has been performed for placement on physician's desk for review.
- For our foreign patients, coordinate their appointments with other physicians (e.g., eye, dental, echocardiogram).
- May have to pick up a medical record for signature and then return to appropriate station.
- Maintain a copy of lectures presented by my boss and then update periodically with changes in outline.
- Keep physician's CV up to date.

- Coordinate meetings for my boss that he has to attend as well as those where he is a member of the committee.
- Arrange for weekend coverage if my boss is not available.

To work in a medical environment, you need to be well organized, have good keyboarding and computer skills, be well versed in spelling, be flexible, have good telephone manners, have a pleasant approach, and be able to think and plan ahead. As you remain in this position, you keep learning and assume more and more responsibility.

If you are interested in a profession in the medical environment, I advise you to continue your education and enroll in a medical secretarial/administrative curriculum for at least a two-year degree and more, if possible. In this type of program, you will learn medical terminology, which would be very beneficial, and clinical procedures, too.

Technical

A technical secretary works for a scientist or an engineer, employers who are generally found in the laboratory rather than in the office. Therefore, the secretary is more of an administrative assistant who is in charge of organizing and implementing most of the office routines. In addition to the usual secretarial duties, the technical secretary prepares most of the correspondence from composing to mailing; maintains the technical library; and gathers, types, and edits materials for scientific papers. The engineering secretary checks specifications in contracts against standards and orders the materials that meet the specifications.

Opportunities are available for the technical secretary who has the following qualifications: knowledge of technology and vocabulary relevant to a specific field, familiarity with mathematical and/or engineering symbols, skills in formatting and keyboarding statistical tables, and high standards of performance in production of technical reports. A good knowledge of and interest in mathematics and science contribute to job satisfaction and success. Besides work in professional offices, jobs are available in industry. Some of the fields for which you can prepare as a technical secretary are in electronics, communications, aerospace, nuclear energy, and ecology.

Educational

Educational secretaries may work in a variety of institutions: private or public elementary, intermediate, or high school; two- or four-year college; and university. If you like working in an educational environment, then you also may have a choice of location. Do you prefer a small town, a large city, or a college town?

School secretaries may work directly with administrators and teachers. They meet and talk with parents, business leaders, visitors, community representatives, and board members. Duties of the position may range from taking dictation and keyboarding correspondence and documents to taking minutes of meetings, preparing governmental reports, and ordering and distributing supplies.

Public schools in some cities require applicants for positions to pass an examination. Therefore, you should investigate this requirement in the area where you wish to find a job.

Jan Barr, secretary to the supervisor of maintenance for the Frederick County Public Schools in Maryland, believes that secretaries need to develop exceptional interpersonal skills, keep up with technology, attend workshops and seminars, and network with professional colleagues.

Private Secretarial Service

For secretaries who wish to operate their own businesses, secretarial services might be the answer. These firms perform a wide range of services for the public such as keyboarding correspondence, reports, proposals, manuals, repetitive letters, database input, and graphs on a microcomputer; composing, formatting, and typing resumes; taking telephone and tape transcription; handling mail (folding, stuffing, sealing, affixing postage); printing labels; notarizing documents; and handling facsimile transmission. To run a business successfully, you need good marketing and managing skills, as well as the ability to determine charges for different types of projects. Pricing jobs is not uniform in all districts; therefore, you need to be able to determine overhead, expenses, cost of equipment, insurance, and supplies. In addition, you need to be knowledgeable about the geographical area in which you are rendering these services. Such a business can be home-based—known as electronic cottages—can be conducted in a storefront, or can be located in a professional building. This is an excellent small business venture for individuals who were secretaries at one time, for they have the right mix of technical, administrative, and interpersonal skills.

What are some of the advantages for the user of these services? The owner of a newly established business who doesn't have the cash flow yet can use these services when needed; it is less expensive than increasing clerical staff; and the customer is charged only for productive time.

Secretarial services as a business has grown so tremendously in the past few years that companies performing these services have organized a professional association as a forum for exchanging ideas and keeping updated on trends in business and technology.

Public Stenographer

The public stenographer is another kind of service rendered to the public by secretaries who wish to run their own business. The offices usually are located in a hotel near prospective employers who need special services in a hurry. Public stenographers serve only those who bring work to them; and because they usually do only small jobs for a traveling population of employers, they can charge rather high rates for piecework. Public stenographers are usually also notary publics, those authorized by the state to witness signatures. For this service they receive a small fee. Much of their work is of a legal nature, and secretaries contemplating careers as public stenographers should be experienced in legal work.

The major advantages of becoming a public stenographer are freedom from supervision and a wide variety of work assignments. One never knows what type of job will be brought in. You can make a very good salary if you are located in a high-paying area. The disadvantages of becoming a public stenographer are the instability of employment and the possibility of low income during holiday periods and slack seasons, or of working in a poor location. Public stenography demands a high degree of skill and flexibility, for each new dictator is different, with unique demands and requirements.

Court Reporter

The opportunities in court reporting are varied and plentiful. It is a highly challenging profession for a person with a knowledge of specialized terminology in the legal, medical, insurance, and engineering fields. The court reporter must also be a good communicator, computer literate, well organized, able to meet deadlines, and work well under pressure.

In this position, the reporter records verbatim statements made at legal proceedings at the city, state, and federal levels and presents their record in the official transcript. There are also freelance reporters who record depositions, or out-of-court testimony for attorneys, as well as take proceedings of meetings and conventions. With modern technology, most reporters now dictate notes on magnetic tapes that a typist can transcribe later. An increasing number of reporters have begun to use Computer-Aided Transcription (CAT). This simply means that a computer is used to transcribe the reporter's stenotype notes that were captured electronically in digital form. The transcript is edited on the computer, which also functions at this level as a word processor.

Business-oriented individuals have been establishing court-reporting firms, a growing industry to serve the legal community. They hire certified reporters, transcribers, and support personnel. Governmental court reporters qualify by examination. However, if your preference is private industry, then you may wish to apply for a position with a reporting corporation.

You may wish to note the trends in court reporting that reflect a compositional change toward increased feminization. Almost 86 percent are women. Of the two-thirds of the court reporters who are freelance workers, 88 percent are women.

Set your goals if you want to become a court reporter. It requires two to four years of technical training and state certification in some jurisdictions. For more details, you may contact Central Michigan University where they have a B.A.A. degree major in court and conference reporting.

CERTIFICATION AND LICENSING

Both the Professional Secretaries International and the National Association of Legal Secretaries sponsor examinations to certify secretaries. The purpose of each of these organizations will be explained later.

A secretary who earns certification is usually a highly motivated person who has superior skills and knowledge. This is viewed by other professionals and employers as a level of achievement that warrants recognition. For secretaries, certification is equal in importance to the CPA designation for accountants. Therefore, if you want to reach the highest level in the secretarial profession, then you should work toward this achievement.

Certified Professional Secretary (CPS)

The CPS is the registered service mark of the Certified Professional Secretary and is the international standard of measurement used to denote secretarial proficiency. Applicants for this rating must pass a one-day, three-part examination that is administered twice a year, in May and November, by the Institute for Certification, a department of the Professional Secretaries International. To date, more than fifty-four thousand secretaries have attained this certification. Candidates must meet minimum requirements in education and secretarial employment experience. To be eligible to take the CPS examination, a secretary must have from two to four years of full-time experience.

The July 9, 1998, PSI Home Page Association News discussed guidelines for eligibility to take the examination:

- Four-year college graduate with a bachelor's degree, two years of verified secretarial experience.
- Two-year college graduate with an associate degree, three years of verified secretarial experience.
- High-school diploma, four years of verified secretarial experience.

Students in two- and four-year colleges may take the examination during their last year; however, they will not be certified until they have acquired the secretarial experience.

The examination is based on an analysis of secretarial activities and is administered in centers located in the United States, Canada, Puerto Rico, and Jamaica. The three parts of the examination and the focus of questions in each section are described as follows:

Part 1: Finance and Business Law (120 questions; 2 hours 30 minutes)

- Measures the secretary's knowledge of principles of *business law* as they may operate in daily work.
- Measures knowledge of the elements of the *accounting* cycle; ability to analyze financial accounts, to perform arithmetical operations

associated with accounting; computing interest and discounts; and summarizing and interpreting financial data.
- Measure an understanding of *economics* and the basic concepts underlying business operations.

Part 2: Office Systems and Administration (150 questions; 2 hours)

- Measures proficiency in subject matters related to *office administration.*
- Measures skills in written *business communications* (editing, abstracting, and preparing communications in final format).
- Tests secretary's knowledge and responsibilities associated with *office technology:* office systems, applications, communications media, and records management.

Part 3: Management (150 questions; 2 hours)

- In *Behavioral Science in Business and Human Resources,* it measures the candidate's understanding of principles of human relations and of self, peers, subordinates, and superiors; it focuses on the fundamentals of one's own needs and motivations, nature of conflict, problem-solving techniques, leadership styles, and understanding of the informal organization.
- In *Management,* organizations and principles of management are the focus.

Many employers have recognized the professionalism, broad range of knowledge, and upgraded skills achieved by certified secretaries. The comment below demonstrates the reasons many executives are interested in certified professional secretaries.

Dave Pylipow, Director of Employee Relations, Hallmark Cards, Incorporated, states: "In today's competitive environment, it's important to have employees who are well educated, can adapt to change, and can initiate change. To earn the CPS rating, secretaries have to study a wide variety of material and gain a broader education. This equips them to effectively handle a bigger array of problems, to initiate change, and to develop innovative ideas."

Many firms encourage secretaries to enroll in the CPS program by offering company reimbursement programs for tuition fees, textbooks, preparatory courses, and examination charges; others offer a monetary bonus and awards. Some give priority for managerial positions to certified secretaries, and others give a salary increase or a one-grade promotion. CPS holders earn an average of $2,228 per year more than office professionals without it, according to the 1997 PSI Membership Profile.

Because of the difficulty of the examination, secretaries who prepare for it devote many hours or even years to preparation. Some colleges give credit for passing this examination and encourage CPSs to complete their formal education. Each college establishes its own criteria for awarding degree credit.

Information on the CPS examination, application, and study materials can be ordered from the Institute for Certifying Secretaries, Department of Professional Secretaries International, 10502 NW Ambassador Drive, P.O. Box 20404, Kansas City, Missouri 64195-0404.

Professional Legal Secretary (PLS)

Certification as a Professional Legal Secretary also can be attained after having worked in this capacity for at least five years and having passed a high-level two-day, seven-part examination that is given in colleges and universities throughout the United States. This examination is administered by the PLS Certifying Board of the National Association of Legal Secretaries (International), (NALS), which consists of two attorneys who are members of the American Bar Association, two educators, and four members of NALS who are PLSs. This examination covers all phases of legal work, and the contents measure the skills, knowledge, and techniques needed to work in a law office. Candidates are examined in the following areas:

1. *Written communication skills and knowledge.* Tests language abilities (grammar, word usage, punctuation, capitalization, spelling, composition, and word division).

2. *Ethics.* Evaluates ability to handle problem situations involving contacts with employer, clients, the public, and coworkers. Ethical considerations are included.

3. *Office procedures.* Measures general administrative ability of secretary in handling the mail and telephone; selecting office supplies and equipment; using sources of information; applying computer technology; and understanding of word processing equipment.

4. *Accounting.* Measures knowledge of general banking and financial activities as well as accounting theory and terminology.

5. *Legal knowledge and procedures.* Focuses on legal terms, legal procedures, legal bibliography, and basic information about preparation of legal documents.

6. *Exercise of judgment.* Evaluates examinee's decision-making ability.

7. *Legal secretarial skills.* Tests skill in following instructions and in taking and preparing legal documents.

If you are interested in legal secretarial employment, then pursue certification, for the PLS is a testimony of competence in your profession. It is the key that opens doors. For further information about the Professional Secretarial Programs, write to the National Association of Legal Secretaries (International), 314 East Third Street, Suite 210, Tulsa, Oklahoma 74120 (918-582-5188).

Accredited Professional Legal Secretary (ALS)

NALS developed this program for individuals at the apprentice level. To become accredited as a legal secretary, you must pass a one-day, six-hour, three-part examination that is offered four times a year, in March, June, September, and December. The three parts of the examination are the following:

Part 1: Written Communication, Comprehension, and Application
Part 2: Office Administration, Legal Terminology, and Accounting
Part 3: Ethics, Human Relations, and Applied Office Procedures

Passing the examination successfully will demonstrate the various skills that are required in a legal environment: perform business communication tasks, maintain office records and calendars, prioritize multiple tasks, understand office equipment and procedures, know legal terminology and document preparation, solve accounting problems, and follow law office protocol as prescribed by ethical codes. The examination is scored under the direction of the NALS Legal Secretary Certifying Board that is composed of four members, four non-NALS members who are lawyers and educators, and the NALS president. Successful candidates earn a certificate that is valid for five years, and certification may be extended one year for every twenty hours of continuing legal education up to a maximum of three years.

Board Certified Civil Trial Legal Secretary

In specialized areas such as litigation and probate, NALS administers an examination that confers the designation Board Certified Civil Trial Legal Secretary. The applicant must have five years of law-related experience and pass the examination.

Certified Medical Assistant (CMA)

The medical secretary can strive to achieve the Certified Medical Assistant designation that certifies professional competence of individuals. The American Association of Medical Assistants, in cooperation with the National Board of Medical Examiners, which serves as educational test consultant, sponsors this examination. It is given twice yearly at many test centers nationwide. In addition to this general certification, specialty certification in administrative (CMA-A) can be achieved. The examination tests general, medical, administrative, and clinical knowledge. For information on these programs, write to The American Association of Medical Assistants, Inc., 20 North Wacker Drive, Suite 1575, Chicago, Illinois 60606.

PROFESSIONAL SECRETARIAL ORGANIZATIONS

International Association of Administrative Professionals

The International Association of Administrative Professionals (as of August 1, 1998) formerly the Professional Secretaries International (PSI), is the world's leading organization for secretaries and has seven hundred chapters and more than forty thousand members on five continents and in more than sixty-four countries. This organization sponsors seminars and workshops at the local, state, and national levels that are organized to develop the personal and professional expertise of secretaries. The organization sponsors a Future Secretaries Association Program, mostly at the high school level, to inform students about the secretarial profession and to interest them in entering the field. Since 1986, the Collegiate Secretaries International has become a student association of PSI under the directorship of the Institute for Educating Secretaries. As you read previously in the chapter, the Certified Professional Secretaries

(CPS) program is one of its major activities. The Research and Educational Foundation provides funds for projects that benefit secretaries, management, and the educational field. In addition, the organization publishes nine issues per year of *The Secretary,* which is mailed to all members.

National Association of Legal Secretaries (NALS)

Legal secretaries are eligible for membership in the National Association of Legal Secretaries (International), NALS, which has more than six thousand members nationwide. Its mission statement reads that it "is dedicated to enhancing the competencies and contributions of members in the legal services profession." It accomplishes its mission and supports the public interest through the following:

- continuing legal education and resource materials
- networking opportunities at the local, state, regional, and national levels
- commitment to a Code of Ethics and professional standards
- professional certification programs and designations

As you read previously in this chapter, the organization sponsors a professional examination and certifying program. You may be asking yourself how you will benefit from being a NALS member. Most important is to make friends and contacts in the profession with whom you may share ideas and experiences. You also receive a copy of the *NALS Law Magazine* four times a year. As a member, you may attend seminars and educational programs held locally and throughout the United States. The Continuing Legal Education Council plans programs on the national level.

U.S. and Canadian Organizations for Medical Secretaries

Medical assistants should become members of the American Association of Medical Assistants. It is an association of individuals including medical secretaries, receptionists, medical office managers, and other medical professionals who work in health care environments. The organization is dedicated to the professional advancement of its constituents.

The organization has more than four hundred chapters with a nationwide membership over twelve thousand. As a member, you are entitled to participate in their continuing education services, usually seminars and workshops, for which you can earn Continuing Education Unit (CEU) credit. Another way to earn CEU credit is by successfully completing examinations that accompany the Guided Study Programs. These are home study courses that enable medical assistants to work independently at their own rate of speed. Three courses are now available: Law for the Medical Office, Human Relations, and Urinalysis Today.

An official bimonthly journal, *The Professional Medical Assistant,* and the *AAMA Network,* a quarterly newsletter, are other benefits of membership.

Because of the nature of the profession, the organization recognizes that members face ethical dilemmas daily; therefore, they developed the AAMA Code of Ethics, which is part of the organization's bylaws. The responsibilities enumerated within are service for the dignity of humanity, respect for confidentiality, maintenance of the high honor and principles of the profession, continued study to improve knowledge and skills of medical assistants, and participation in services to improve the community.

Another professional medical organization to join is the American Association of Medical Transcriptionists, who are usually employed in medical institutions.

In Ontario, Canada, medical secretaries are eligible for membership in the Ontario Medical Secretaries Association (O. M. S. A.). This is a provincial organization whose primary goal is to expand the knowledge base of its members and keep them abreast of rapidly changing office methods and equipment. The association sponsors a certification program for qualified applicants to achieve professional status as a Certified Medical Secretary (CMS).

National Association of Educational Office Personnel

Educational secretaries may belong to the National Association of Educational Office Personnel. This group works for increased recognition for educational office personnel. It sponsors a Professional Standards

Program (PSP) to encourage members to grow professionally and to keep up to date in the profession and field of education. It also has an awards program in which it honors outstanding administrators and office professionals, individuals for distinguished service, and affiliated associations for outstanding newsletters and magazines. A benefit along with membership is *The National Educational Secretary,* which is published four times a year.

National Association of Secretarial Services (NASS)

The National Association of Secretarial Services (NASS) represents secretarial service owners and managers. It has twelve hundred members and forty state groups. Active membership is granted to businesses that are engaged in full-time services. The association publishes a newsletter that includes diverse articles pertaining to the membership's type of business. It also holds workshops and seminars and shares referrals and training. For information about this organization, you may write to 3637 Fourth Street North, Suite 330, St. Petersburg, Florida 33704-1336 (813-823-3646 or Fax: 813-894-4277).

SALARIES

The changing times, increasing office automation, and innovative business practices have affected the secretarial work environment, but it has not resulted in a lack of demand for qualified secretaries. Job openings should be plentiful for qualified, experienced secretaries, primarily due to replacement of those who transfer to other occupations or leave for other reasons. In the 1998 *Occupational Outlook Quarterly,* the statistics indicated that 25,000 more general secretaries will be employed by 2006, above the 1996 figure of 3,403,000 that were employed. Legal and medical secretaries will show a major growth rate.

In terms of pay, workers in larger establishments generally have a pay advantage over those working in smaller organizations. Earnings of administrative workers showed very little variation by establishment size, 3 percent of each other—from 1 percent below established categories with 1,000 workers to 2 percent above in establishments with 1,000 to 2,499 workers. Among the secretaries, one of the most populous clerical occupations, secretarial level III earnings were nearly identical in all establishment size categories, varying only by $3 from the mean of $547 per week.

Salaries for secretaries vary greatly, reflecting differences in level of skill, experience, and responsibility. In addition, salaries in different parts of the country vary depending on demand, current salary scales of industry, and availability of personnel. Generally, compensation in large cities is higher than in small towns, and the earnings on the East and West coasts are above the earnings in the Midwest or South. Those cities that offer the highest salaries are New York, Boston, and Los Angeles with Washington, DC and San Francisco close behind. Also, salaries of secretaries tend to be highest in transportation, legal services, and public utilities. Certification in the field is generally recognized by an increase in salary. It is significant that secretarial salaries reach a high point that exceeds those of all other clerical positions.

The figures in Table 13 that was researched and gathered throughout the United States by Office Team will give you some idea of 1998 annual salaries earned by secretaries compared to other office workers.

Table 13. 1998 U.S. SALARY RANGES

Administrative/Secretarial Personnel	
Title	1998
Administrative Assistant/Secretary I	$19,000–$24,000
Administrative Assistant/Secretary II	22,000– 35,000
Executive Assistant/Secretary I	25,000– 32,750
Executive Assistant/Secretary II	31,250– 44,000
Specialized Medical Secretary	26,000– 36,000
Word Processor	18,500– 23,000
Executive Word Processor	21,000– 32,000
Office Manager (up to five years experience)	24,000– 31,000
Office Manager (five-plus years experience)	32,000– 41,000
Receptionist/Administrative Assistant	19,750– 25,000
Desktop Publishing Specialist	25,500– 36,500

Source: 1998 Office Team Salary Guide

Table 14. AVERAGE WEEKLY SALARIES FOR SECRETARIES IN
SELECTED METROPOLITAN AREAS

Secretaries	U.S.	Northeast	South	Northwest	West
LEVEL I	$393	$426	$377	$418	$392
Private industry	405	434	393	423	386
Manufacturers	448	458	415	498	—
Service producing	394	426	386	401	379
Transportation and utilities	423	—	421	—	—
State and local govt.	376	409	360	409	—
LEVEL II	481	503	446	474	530
Private industry	488	500	471	471	521
Manufacturing	510	518	486	492	546
Service producing	483	497	466	465	513
Transportation and utilities	508	—	502	530	490
State and local govt.	467	514	417	480	546
LEVEL III	560	587	525	560	580
Private industry	566	584	546	560	575
Manufacturing	584	596	568	592	584
Service producing	556	580	532	543	568
Transportation and utilities	580	639	547	608	563
State and local govt.	541	601	475	558	596
LEVEL IV	667	693	673	644	681
Private industry	675	692	647	651	689
Manufacturing	684	693	682	651	708
Service producing	668	691	637	651	676
Transportation and utilities	695	744	647	724	697
State and local govt.	633	701	547	609	662
LEVEL V	810	828	754	822	812
Private industry	817	829	767	825	820
Manufacturing	815	804	745	868	829
Service producing	816	848	768	773	812
Transportation and utilities	838	—	772	—	—
State and local govt.	751	816	705	—	772

Source: 1996 National Summary of Occupational Compensation Survey, March 1998, Bulletin 2497

You will also be interested in glancing at the average weekly salaries in the different parts of the country, as illustrated in Table 14. This might be a factor to consider when you look for a job.

If you wish to relocate, notice the difference in salary between the East and the West coasts, particularly between New York City and Sacramento (see Table 15). Whereas the average weekly income for all secretaries in New York is $600, in Sacramento it is $505. Similarly, at the highest level, a secretary earns an average of $848 in the East; on the West Coast, it is slightly lower, $829. In service industries in the Northeast, you can earn as high as $848; in the West, $812.

You will also want to bear in mind that salary differentials may reflect the increased cost of living in a given area. Investigate the fixed expenses of rent, taxes, and other significant items that may be higher than the area in which you presently live before you consider a move. A list of the expenses where you presently live can be used as a starting point. You can request information from the chamber of commerce where you are thinking of moving, from friends, and from such organizations as church groups, civic organizations, schools, and banks.

CANADIAN SALARIES

The wide range of salaries in Canada, shown in Table 16, depends on region, skill, experience, and responsibilities of the position. Salary figures given below are in Canadian dollars.

The *career program* refers to recent graduates who completed a two-year community college. The average salary for all of these fields of

Table 15. AVERAGE WEEKLY AND ANNUAL EARNINGS OF SECRETARIES IN SELECTED CITIES

Area	Weekly	Annual
New York, Northern New Jersey, Long Island	$600	$30,757
Milwaukee-Racine, Wisconsin	497	25,004
Sacramento-Yolo, California	505	25,690

Source: National Compensation Survey for New York, Northern New Jersey, Long Island, Bulletin 3090–10; Milwaukee-Racine, Wisconsin, Bulletin 3090-31; Sacramento-Yolo, California, Bulletin 3090-9.

study is \$26,700. The *trade/vocational* program that is less than one year shows an average salary of \$24,200. The individuals in the third category, designated as o*thers,* generally work in government and throughout the private sector, including law and medical settings. The average salary in all fields in this group is \$34,900. Full-time earnings by categories are given in Table 16. Note that the spread of salaries is from the lowest to the highest, with the average salary earned in the middle.

Table 16. FULL-TIME EARNINGS BY CATEGORIES

Lowest 10%—Average—Highest 10%

Category	Salary Range (Canadian Dollars)	Average for Field
Career Program (Community College)		**\$26,700**
Secretary-General	\$11,200–\$21,600–\$39,000	
Secretary-Legal	12,900– 23,600– 35,400	
Secretary-Medical	13,800– 25,800– 38,400	
Trade/Vocational College		**\$24,200**
Secretary-Accounting and Bookkeeping	9,100– 19,100– 28,800	
Secretary-General	7,700– 18,900– 30,200	
Secretary-Medical	8,000– 16,900– 24,600	
Secretary-Word Processing	9,800– 18,800– 29,500	
Secretary-Legal	11,300– 20,800– 33,500	
Others		**\$34,900**
Clerical Occupations, General Office Skills	14,900– 27,700– 40,200	
Secretaries, Recorders, and Transcriptionists	15,500– 28,600– 37,500	
Legal Secretaries	17,700– 28,600– 39,400	
Medical Secretaries	15,300– 25,200– 33,300	

Source: *Job Futures,* Volume 1: *Occupational Outlooks;* Volume 2: *Career Outlooks for Graduates*

FRINGE BENEFITS

Although fringe benefits are considered apart from salaries, nevertheless they have a substantial money value. Consider the cost of hospitalization, medical insurance, vacation benefits, life insurance, and retirement plans. The pre-established benefits that were provided by the company are now being replaced in some companies by pick-and-choose plans or *cafeteria* plans, as they are frequently called. Other companies now require employees to pay for a portion of their health coverage. Plans will vary as they are adopted by employers. For example, a firm might give its employees a core of basic benefits, such as those mentioned above; then from another group of options, employees may select benefits up to a maximum amount.

Do not expect all kinds of fringe benefits. Companies are trying to find ways to cut the costs of providing fringe benefits. Be sure you know what your benefits will be when you accept a job.

THE WAGE GAP

In job evaluation studies of a job, the factors measured are the inherent skills of the job, effort needed to perform job, responsibility, and working conditions. Traditionally, clerical work has been performed by women. Although women have been fighting for equality, and some progress has been made, a gap still exists between women's and men's earnings. The good news is that women's pay and a percent of men's pay have increased substantially. In 1976, women earned 69 percent of what men earned on an hourly basis. In 1996, women's earnings were 89 percent of men's, which is a 17 percent increase. The pay of American women working full-time year-round averages 72 cents for each dollar earned by men. If you experience problems with fair pay, contact the Women's Bureau Fair Pay Clearinghouse at (800) 347-3741.

Canadian earnings of men and women. In the office support occupations, more than 95 percent of the employees are women, with the exception of clerical occupations, general office skills, where 76 percent of the workers are women. After glancing at Table 17 on the average earnings of men and women in Canada, you will realize that the average salary for men is considerably higher. Statistics indicate that earnings are lower than the average level in practically all of the office occupations.

Table 17. AVERAGE EARNINGS OF MEN AND WOMEN IN CANADA

	1992	1993	1994	1995
	1992–1995			
Male[1]	$31,042	$30,407	$31,770	$31,053
Female[1]	19,831	19,566	19,784	20,219
Male[2]	41,270	40,441	41,611	40,610
Female[2]	29,669	29,207	29,047	29,700

[1]All earners

[2]Full-year full-time workers

Source: *Canadian Almanac & Directory,* 1998

CHAPTER 6

IS SECRETARIAL WORK FOR YOU?

Secretaries always have and continue to make a difference in today's business world. Changes that affect the office environment are moving at speeds of lightning. To enjoy the career you select, you need to move with the times. You need to develop your skills not only to include the mastery of computer software and the latest technology, but also to develop leadership, organizational, interpersonal, problem-solving, and communication competencies. You need to be flexible, able to adjust to constant change, and understand and enjoy a diverse workforce and the culture employees bring to the workplace. Take advantage of all opportunities to enhance your skills, to gain knowledge, and to make yourself a valuable member of the firm. Keep in mind that secretaries are now assuming many of the responsibilities that were previously in the realm of managers. Since 262,000 positions as clerical supervisors and managers are forecasted to be added between 1996 and 2006, this might be the direction you would like to take for advancement and challenging responsibilities.

When making decisions about a career, you undoubtedly should select one that is satisfying, enjoyable, and at which you can perform well. Some of the factors you should evaluate in selecting a career are your likes and dislikes for certain kinds of work, the opportunities within the field, promotional paths for upward mobility, earning power, socialization, and employment opportunities that exist now as well as in the future.

Probably the single most important advantage in planning a secretarial career is knowing that a great need exists for this category of office work. Even during periods of recession, the demand for secretaries is high because of the tremendous amounts of paperwork that companies must process. As stated in the previous chapter, the job outlook is very good. Another advantage of secretarial work is the diversity of options that are available in selecting executive and administrative work or specialties, such as legal, educational, or medical. Another option is become self-employed and a successful entrepreneur. You can open your own secretarial services establishment or become a freelance transcriptionist.

In addition, alternative schedules to the traditional workday from 9 A.M. to 5 P.M. are now operative in firms across the country. If you are a busy homemaker, you may choose to work part-time, or if you enjoy learning about many companies, you can work as a temporary employee. Still more interesting is flextime for individuals who want to work around family responsibilities. Another advantage is to choose an alternative location for your workplace, a direction in which many firms are now going, rather than the office setting where you normally carried out the responsibilities of the job. See Chapter 4 for more information.

On the bleaker side of the job is the frequent need to work on the weekend. According to the *Steelcase Workplace Index,* a semiannual survey that measures workplace trends in the United States, 73 percent of office employees work on the weekend. Sixty percent work on weekends once a month or more; 42 percent work six to ten hours; 8 percent spend eleven to fifteen hours; 10 percent work sixteen to twenty hours; and 5 percent spend twenty-one or more hours. An employee cannot count on the nine-to-five hours daily. The survey also revealed that 49 percent of office employees work more hours than they did five years ago. This was not graciously accepted by 38 percent who "did it because it was expected of them." "Thirty-seven percent of the respondents indicated they work more because they enjoy it."

TRENDS IN OFFICE ENVIRONMENTS

Dramatic advances in office automation have provided a new world of opportunities for secretarial careers. No longer are jobs necessarily dead-end clerical positions. New avenues of career progression have opened up for individuals who keep updated in skills and knowledge. Secretarial workstations now contain the hardware and software for multifunctional responsibilities such as word processing, data processing, telecommunications, presentation graphics, and spreadsheets. Workstations are integrated through local area networks, and secretaries have access to the Internet and communicate through the use of e-mail. Secretarial job responsibilities are growing and expanding in direct relation to the sophistication of the equipment secretaries are operating.

The rate of growth is good and is opening up more diversified career opportunities that require different attitudes and skills, higher-level decision making and problem-solving abilities, and new knowledge qualifications. A question pertaining to these new designs is: Who will manage these systems? Undoubtedly, the person who will qualify will have to understand the broad concepts of office systems, management, productivity, and personnel administration.

Another trend in office environments that has implications for those who want more meaningful work experiences is the growth of departments of human resources. Management has seen fit to shift its emphasis from the sole use of technology to increase productivity to more efficient use of people. This presupposes good human relationships among staff hierarchy, which ultimately results in greater job satisfaction, a feeling of belonging, and the surfacing of creativity skills that were previously dormant. Organizations have converted their personnel departments into departments of human resources that focus on management of people rather than administration of policies and procedures. In these companies there is an organized effort to match people with jobs. There is an assessment of skills, knowledge, and abilities of personnel; and personal growth is encouraged. Some firms incorporate career counseling and training in their program.

This new direction in organizational management supports the theory that even though office processes are automated, it is human intelligence and motivated, competent personnel that are needed to communicate and expand on that information.

With the realization by management that personnel is one of the key areas in reaching the goals of office automation also comes the need to improve work environments. Work space, equipment, and furniture are now designed to accommodate the needs of people as well as the task. This has resulted in attractive, landscaped surroundings that serve the psychological and physiological needs of the workers. You need no longer work in a dull, stress-producing environment due to isolation, high noise levels, poor lighting, and hard floors. This whole new area of study in the office, known as ergonomics, is concerned with people's needs.

Steelcase Inc., the world's leading designer and manufacturer of office furniture, was commissioned to work for Owens Corning on a new work culture based on 1. advanced use of technology, 2. enhanced exchange of information, and 3. new levels of interaction. The vision for this new work culture would include self-directed networks of employees who would work collaboratively, using the company's advanced technology. The design developed included open work spaces, private enclosed areas to supplement open spaces, and fully equipped teaming rooms. When finished, the physical environment would allow for more interaction, enhanced communication, better use of technology, and a workplace that stimulates its staff. A survey of more than four hundred of Owens Corning employees found that 60 percent stated productivity had improved, 80 percent are more customer focused, and 75 percent indicated that meetings are more efficient. Another good outcome as noted in the survey was that 88 percent of the employees reported a high level of teaming with departmental coworkers, and 66 percent across departmental boundaries.

Another factor that has impacted the office is the fact that information is now a corporate resource, similar to plant and equipment. Information and communication are becoming almost synonymous terms as we witness the interconnection of machines. Of what value is information unless it is communicated from person to person and from location to location? Therefore, office administration now occupies an area of importance in company goals equal to marketing, finance, and personnel.

ADVANCEMENT OPPORTUNITIES

The number of traditional secretaries began to decrease from the time word processing was first introduced. Secretaries who primarily worked in automated offices began to support more than one principal. With downsizing, they also began to assume many responsibilities formerly performed by managers. Advancement comes with these added responsibilities. According to Professional Secretaries International, "companies are creating a multitude of career paths for persons in office/ administrative professions. Secretaries have moved into training, supervision, desktop publishing, information management, and research." They should have a technical and conceptual knowledge of the field and an understanding of the business operations of the organization.

Interestingly, secretaries were the ones initially trained to become managers of word processing centers.

Women in management is an extremely broad group. They are most likely to be managers in the same field in which there were proportionately more of them employed below the managerial level. Women held three-fourths (75 percent) of all managerial positions in medicine and health. The May 1998 issue on *Facts on Working Women* from the Women's Bureau indicates that secretaries and cashiers are still the occupations where the largest numbers of women are employed. The supply of women qualified for management positions continues to increase as they assume more office management responsibilities, accumulate work experience, and continue their professional education to achieve an appropriate college degree in business, personnel administration, or accounting. According to the U.S. Department of Labor, 262,000 positions as clerical supervisors/managers are predicted to be added between 1996 and 2006. For more information, read From Secretaries to Managers and Mobility in Chapter 2.

Besides supervisory and managerial opportunities, you also have a lateral career option, which is to switch from jobs with one type of responsibility to another, such as from computer operator to trainer. However, if your main goal is to aspire to a managerial position, you would be wise to concentrate on developing the following qualifications: interpersonal relations skills; flexibility in dealing with others and in making efficient changes in operations and procedures; willingness to delegate; ability to direct, guide, and motivate employees; a pleasant, yet assertive personality and enthusiastic attitude; and an understanding of the company, including its goals, its policies, and its philosophies.

Through secretarial work, employees can demonstrate a potential for management responsibilities. This experience in combination with continuing education will open up channels for promotion. Continue to update your knowledge and skills and keep abreast of technological advances by joining professional organizations, by attending seminars and workshops, and by reading current literature in the field. Finally, sometimes even adhering to all of these suggestions will not be promising for you unless you take a positive attitude and view your job as a career rather than a job. This means you must do more than just what is expected of you, and you must plan strategies for reaching certain goals. Opportunity may strike, but some people also make it happen. Accept the challenges that are offered to you, make your desires to advance known to your supervisors and management, and maintain this visibility.

TEAMWORK IS IN!

Autocratic management styles from top-down are beginning to be replaced by self-managed work teams. This type of management enables employees at all levels in an organization to participate and share responsibility for implementing organizational goals. Group work settings support a more participative culture, an enhanced exchange of information, and greater levels of team interaction. Surveys indicate that increased productivity is an offshoot of teamwork. If you are part of an office professional team, you, as well as the other members of your team, must understand what is expected of you—your roles and responsibilities—and how you can make a contribution to the department or firm. Teams are usually involved in the administrative functions of planning, organizing, and complex problem solving; and each member of the team develops the collaborative skills needed to work with the group. As employees gain empowerment as they work in these teams, they learn to manage themselves.

What are the skills and personal qualities that secretaries need to demonstrate as part of a successful team? First and most important is a commitment to company goals. Other skills and qualities are the following:

- communicating frequently with all members of the team and appropriate managers; listening effectively, considering contributions of others, and separating fact from emotions
- identifying and solving problems
- keeping up to date
- suggesting ideas and procedures for implementing them

A secretary and manager can also constitute a team. Gloria Foster, an executive secretary, states that those who take the initiative make things happen: "They recognize opportunities to improve, change, create, and contribute to their work environment." You can use these various means to: familiarize yourself with all aspects of the organization, volunteer for jobs other than what is expected of you in your position, keep learning and add to your storehouse of knowledge, and contribute to a productive and harmonious working environment. Effective teamwork leads to improvement in a company's productive operations and to more satisfied employees who have gained a professional identity within the organization.

IS THERE A PLACE FOR OLDER WORKERS IN THE JOB MARKET?

Some personnel experts believe that workers beyond the age of fifty have a competitive edge in the job market. They usually have had previous experience with several employers and are looked up to as role models by younger workers. The older employee conveys an image of stability. Until recently, mature individuals had been returning to the job market for several reasons: an inflationary economy bringing about a need for additional family income; self-fulfillment; boredom after children grow up; changing social values; and the women's liberation movement.

Some statements made by employers about older workers who are their employees are very complimentary and highlight the positive qualities they possess, such as motivation, care of equipment, and belief that coming to work is a high priority. A survey by the Commonwealth Fund in New York stated in the December 28, 1997, *New York Times* that "...workers over 55 were better than younger workers when it came to work attitude, turnover, and absenteeism."

Despite age, mature individuals have many opportunities to find employment. Many of them, when they first return to the job market, look forward to full-time employment with trepidation, not certain that they will be able to cope with the demands of the job as well as with their personal and family responsibilities. Therefore, some of these mature individuals may opt for temporary or part-time jobs—an expanding mode of employment. Before long, this worker usually adjusts to the workday routine, begins to gain self-confidence, and is ready for a full-time position. With the dearth of qualified secretaries and the thirst for qualified help to fill the positions that go unfilled each year, the returning adult who has a sense of responsibility and loyalty and who possesses good skills should have no difficulty finding and keeping a job. These adults should enlist in continuing education courses to update their skills, abilities, and knowledge.

U.S. Department of Labor statistics indicates that older workers will account for an increasing share of the labor force, and they will be the fastest-growing segment of the labor force. Over the 1996–2006 period, the fifty-five to sixty-four age group is projected to grow 48 percent by 2006. This rate is one-fourth lower than the forty-five to fifty-four age group. During this same period, the labor force aged forty-five to fifty-four adds the most workers, 8.8 million. Another 6.6 million workers are added from those aged fifty-five to sixty-four. In Canada, the proportion of women in the federal public service aged forty-five or older rose in 1997 to 35 percent from 32.5 percent in March 1996. The proportion was lower, however, than that for men aged forty-five or older, which rose to 47.4 percent from 45.6 percent last year.

Many adult training centers, public schools, private business institutions, and colleges have developed one-year certificate programs for the adult who wants to return to school. These adults may enroll in refresher courses or may wish to learn specialized skills needed in offices with modern technology. Some schools even have cooperative work programs where students work in industry for a stipulated period of time each week. This experience enables the mature adult who has been a homemaker for many years to become accustomed to the working environment and to get a broad view of the changes that have occurred.

MISCONCEPTIONS ABOUT SECRETARIAL WORK

There have been many misconceptions about secretarial work that need clarification. These perceptions pertain to poor image, low salaries, women's work concept, and replacement by automation.

Low Esteem of Secretaries

Technological innovations have brought many changes to the secretarial profession and will continue to impact the work secretaries do. In the past, "She is 'only' a secretary" or she is "my gal Friday" were images of a secretary attacked by the women's liberation movement. Because of this image, many qualified individuals shied away from entering the field. However, through the hard work of professional secretarial organizations and changes brought about in business with the advent of word processing environments, which created secretarial specialists as well as supervisory and managerial positions for secretaries, this image began to fade.

As you read in previous chapters, new areas of responsibility have developed for secretaries that involve the mastery of word processing, spreadsheet, and database management software. Some are even using desktop publishing to design brochures, manuals, and fliers. Also, with downsizing, many secretaries began to perform managerial duties. With the emphasis on human resources, some are also becoming organizational team members. Those individuals who are actively involved need to demonstrate the ability to analyze problems and make decisions, to exhibit professional behaviors, and to use good oral and written communication skills.

Women are becoming more vocal and self-assertive and are demanding respect as professionals. They want responsibility and wish to advance in their careers. Today's secretary is better educated than those of previous decades and will not be relegated to low status. In fact, executives themselves are realizing that qualified secretaries are harder to replace than good executives. In essence, the secretary is a valued staff member of the office; and as positions become more responsible, secretaries will receive greater recognition.

Title changes are also being made to improve the image of the secretary, and it is becoming quite common to hear "assistant," "administrative assistant," "administrative support staff" and "executive assistant," rather than "secretary." Some companies are developing job descriptions to reflect increased responsibilities. In some firms, senior executives and partners still want secretaries with good shorthand and keyboarding skills, although performing administrative duties is a major part of the job. In effect, the "executive secretary" performs similar tasks. In information processing environments, however, the responsibilities are expanding to include a knowledge of information systems. All secretaries now have terminals on their desks, and they certainly know how to retrieve information stored in the computer and how to send communications electronically. Whether known as a secretary or administrative assistant, tasks may be similar. Perhaps some day there will be more definitive titles based on levels of responsibility. Nevertheless, you, the secretary, no matter what your title, must believe in the job and in yourself.

Salaries

Another misconception about secretaries is that they are paid low salaries. The Bureau of Labor Statistics reported in June 1996 that the average weekly salaries ranged from $393 for Level I secretaries to $810 for Level V. Compare these earnings with those of computer operators whose compensation ranges from $387 per week for Level I to $820 for Level V. Accounting clerks averaged $321 a week for Level I to $553 for Level IV, while personnel assistants received weekly salaries from $342 for Level I to $607 for Level IV. Another look at some metropolitan districts indicates that in the Northeast area, top-level secretaries can earn as much as $828 per week, and in the Midwest $822 weekly. The low average point in these cities is $426 and $418 respectively.[1]

Secretarial salaries have been rising each year. Also be aware of the fact that the demand for secretaries is still strong, and that a dearth of qualified individuals exists for those who possess higher-level skills. All indications are that there is a bright, exciting future for this career field.

Women's Work

There has been a movement for women to leave traditionally female occupations for those that were once exclusively for males. As for males entering the secretarial profession, they are beginning to see the opportunities and satisfaction that they can derive, particularly with the invasion of technology and systems in office environments. The future may be more promising, and we may see more males entering the profession for the following reasons: as firms delete the word *secretary* from titles, men will not feel the "stigma" attached to the job and become candidates for available positions; jobs are available now and projected to continue in the future; automation is creating many opportunities for advancement; challenges for systems and innovation and creativity exist; and supervisory and managerial positions with varied titles and responsibilities appeal to the upwardly mobile.

Finley A. Lanier, Jr., who began his career as a secretary in a word processing department and has been in the profession for a long time,

---

[1]*Occupational Compensation Survey,* Bureau of Labor Statistics, 1996, Bulletin 2497.

states: "The profession was intriguing since very few males sought entrance, and I wanted to secure a future with skills that would be helpful in landing a job. I have found it to be rather challenging and stressful at times. Serving others and being on top of things and networking with counterparts are only a few of the rewards achieved from this career. When one can take pride in the accomplishments in a day's work and know that as a result you have added a dimension to the situation, this really is gratifying." Some advice Lanier gives to be successful is that "a secretary must stay out of office politics, avoid arguments, and remember that you are there to serve a purpose and to get the job done. That is the only thing that matters."

Another interesting factor that might reverse this "female occupation" is the trend toward workstations where executives are now being forced to perform keyboarding functions once exclusively within the secretary's domain. Reluctantly, executives are learning to "key-in" their own requests on their terminals. This, too, should bring about a different set of attitudes about secretarial work.

Impact of Automation on Employment of Secretaries

According to the 1998–99 *Occupational Outlook Handbook,* job openings for secretaries should be plentiful, especially for well-qualified and experienced secretaries. Employment growth for medical secretaries will be faster than average, and for legal secretaries, average growth. Although there will be a small decline due to automation in general secretarial positions, the need exists for replacement of workers who leave or transfer to other occupations. Equally important is the generation of new job opportunities in several rapidly growing industries, such as personnel supply, computer and data processing, and management and public relations.

Neither automation nor economic factors will have an adverse impact on employment of secretaries. The demand will continue to be strong. What will happen will be changes in the role of the secretary both in traditional and automated environments. Undoubtedly, there will be demands for secretaries with different kinds of needs and personal characteristics with the trend toward telecommuting, or working at home (see Chapter 4 for more detailed information).

CHAPTER 7

EDUCATIONAL PREPARATION FOR SECRETARIAL/OFFICE PROFESSIONAL POSITIONS

Between 1996 and 2006, the projections of the U.S. Department of Labor indicate that there will be about 250,000 more college graduates entering the labor force each year than there will be college-level jobs. This means that 18 percent of new college graduates may not be able to find college-level jobs. The logical question to ask then is why are so many high school graduates enrolling in college to earn a degree? Mark Mittelhauser, an economist in the Office of Employment projects believes that college graduates are favored in the labor market. They earn more money and experience lower unemployment rates than workers without a degree. The unemployment rate of college graduates in 1996, which was 2.4 percent, was less than half of the absenteeism rate for high school graduates, 5.4 percent.

Approximately thirty-three million college graduates were employed in 1996 in the United States. Two groups, the professional specialty occupation and the executive, administrative, and managerial occupations accounted for two-thirds of the college-level employment, 14 million jobs and 8.4 million, respectively. The administrative support occupations, including secretaries, clerical supervisors, and managers, accounted for an additional 2.6 million workers.

Many new openings created by growth reflects a related phenomenon—educational upgrading. With restructuring and change, many workers assume new responsibilities. Statistics support this statement. Of the 750,000 college-level job openings that were due to projected growth,

40 percent of these openings are due to upgrading between 1996 and 2006.

Today, as well as in the past, the minimum educational requirement for an entry-level secretarial position is graduation from high school. However, with the impact that technology has had on office procedures, systems, and responsibilities now assumed by secretaries, employers generally prefer hiring those candidates who have a solid foundation in secretarial and computer skills and are proficient in the use of the English language—spelling, grammar, punctuation, vocabulary. In addition, flexibility, attitude and willingness to accept change in all facets of the work environment, pleasing personality, poise, good interpersonal skills, and use of diplomacy in human relations are qualities that give the prospective employee a competitive edge over others. For supervisory and managerial positions, postsecondary education is desirable. The use of initiative, discretion, and good judgment, as well as the ability to organize daily activities, prioritize, manage time effectively, and be a wise decision maker are traits sought in candidates.

Although you read in the previous paragraph that the minimum requirement for a secretarial position is graduation from high school, you need to know the background of individuals who are already working in these positions. You need to prepare yourself to compete with the population looking for employment.

In jobs where a degree is not required, college graduates who either do not find employment in their field or who choose to make a career switch will be a source of employment for these jobs. Therefore, the competition will be keener; employers may look upon these college graduates more favorably, particularly as skills needed in secretarial positions become more complex. Some employers actually inflate the educational requirement for some jobs because of the abundance of college graduates looking for work and because they anticipate grooming graduates for administrative and managerial positions.

Specific hiring requirements for secretaries vary from firm to firm; however, many companies require a keying speed of sixty-five words per minute (wpm) and above seventy wpm for individuals in word processing areas. A knowledge of shorthand is an asset in being offered a well-paying secretarial job, particularly during periods when competition is keen and in large firms where higher-level executives and senior partners request it. Some employers may still use shorthand testing as a screening device for a better-qualified applicant. More will be said about the need for shorthand in the following section titled Is Shorthand Obsolete?

A continuous need has existed for specialized secretaries in legal, medical, and technical organizations. In these specialties, you need a firm grounding in terminology, an understanding of the field, and knowledge of office procedures used in the specific kind of environment.

In addition to the general secretarial and specialized skills and knowledge already mentioned, good organizational ability and knowledge of software applications, such as word processing, spreadsheet, database management, scanners, and information storage systems, will give you the leading edge in a competitive job market. The continuing changes occurring in office environments because of technology affect equipment and procedures as well as skill and knowledge requirements. Concomitantly, new career paths and positions continue to be created that call for different combinations of skills, attitudes, and knowledge. Alert individuals who consider education as an ongoing process and as an integral part of the job will become prime candidates for these openings.

IS SHORTHAND OBSOLETE?

Opinions vary about the need for shorthand. Some believe it is necessary for secretarial employment; and since it is no longer used extensively, others believe it is becoming an archaic skill. Shorthand dictation is still used in some offices, particularly by executives who became accustomed to working routinely with a specific individual. Shorthand is used on a pretty steady basis by secretaries and office professionals for telephone messages, recording instructions, and taking minutes of meetings. Having a good shorthand skill is really a plus. When checking the help-wanted ads in *The New York Times* under the general categories of "executive secretary" and "secretary," a small percentage of the ads specify shorthand. However, a good number of higher-level executives and senior partners in law firms require shorthand. Individuals who are proponents of shorthand state that those individuals with shorthand skills average approximately an 18 percent higher salary than those

without it. Job seekers with shorthand skills have a competitive edge over those lacking this skill in being hired in the better salaried jobs.

The above statements attest to the fact that the demand for shorthand has decreased considerably for general secretarial work; however, it is not yet obsolete. It is still a requirement in some higher-level administrative executive secretarial positions and in legal positions with partners. Shorthand skill is a plus and will open doors to positions in the executive suite.

SECRETARIAL/ADMINISTRATIVE ASSISTANT PROGRAMS OF STUDY

Secretarial education continues to be offered; however, the curriculum or program designation varies in each school. Courses of study are offered in high school vocational training centers and one- and two-year programs in business schools, vocational-technical institutions, and community colleges. In degree-granting institutions, students need to complete liberal arts as well as specialized courses. Review the curricula from the different schools and districts that are included in the text that follows.

High School Programs

In the past, schools in a particular district would offer similar programs for the secretarial major. However, there is no consistency now in New York State, and requirements for liberal arts and business courses vary from school to school because of the added state requirements in the academic areas. This has affected the number of electives that can be selected from the field of business. Each school district is now tailoring these electives to meet its local needs.

In schools equipped with personal computers, students generally learn to keyboard on this equipment. In Nanuet High School in Nanuet, New York, which has the latest technology, students learn the computer keyboard in the first semester. The students who are majoring in the secretarial field take a second semester of keyboarding, where in addition to developing their keyboarding skills, they do production work that includes correspondence and reports. Some basic English is also taught. In the third semester, business computer applications are presented and students learn to do word processing, set up a database, and learn a spreadsheet.

Included in the instructions are rough drafts, endnotes, superscripts, and other types of notations. Advanced computer work is presented in the fourth semester, in which software packages are introduced: for example, Word, Powerpoint, Excel, Desktop Publishing, and Print Shop.

The Business Education Department in Ramapo Senior High School, Spring Valley, New York, which serves a large population, offers a Three-Unit Sequence and Model Five-Unit Sequences. Overall, the department offers thirty courses from which students have certain choices, based on the sequence they elect to follow. Some of them are computer courses, including keyboarding, word processing, spreadsheets, and desktop publishing; finance and law courses; marketing-management courses; mathematics courses; speedwriting; Retail Store Academy; Work Experience Program; and Career Exploration Internship Program (CEIP). As you review the curriculum below, note that "s" stands for semester.

BUSINESS-MARKETING EDUCATION SEQUENCES
RAMAPO SENIOR HIGH SCHOOL

Three-Unit Sequence Options

As the World Changes 1 & 2 (Introduction to Occupations)

or

As the World Changes 1 (S) and CEIP 1 (S)

and one of the following:

Computers in Business (BA/BCA)
Personal Keyboarding and Business Communications
Keyboarding

plus one of the following full-year courses:

Accounting
Business Communications and Personal Keyboarding
Business Law
College Accounting
College Business Law
Computers in Business (BA/BCA)
Computer Spreadsheets 1 & 2
Keyboarding
Principles of Marketing

Record Keeping (Financial Information Processing)
Word Processing 1 & 2 (Electronic Information Processing)

Model Five-Unit Sequences

As the World Changes 1 & 2 (Introduction to Occupations)
Personal Keyboarding and Business Communications
Computers in Business (BA/BCA)

plus any two courses listed below:

Marketing Cluster	**Financial Cluster**	**Information Cluster**
Principles of Marketing	Accounting	Computers in Business
Cooperative Work Experience	College Accounting	Computer Spreadsheets 1 & 2
CEIP	Business Law	Word Processing 1 & 2
	College Business Law	Cooperative Work Experience
	Cooperative Work Experience	CEIP
	CEIP	

Alternatives to the traditional 40-minute class period have been implemented in various high schools. Some now have block programs of two or three periods so that business situations can be simulated. Under this reorganization, students can complete tasks originated within the time frame, rather than having to stop a project that is only partially completed. Some innovations also include simulated experiences in advanced keyboarding and office procedures classes. The advantage to this arrangement is that students see the interrelationships between different office jobs being performed. One of the benefits students derive in these simulated experiences is training in human relations, an aspect frequently neglected in more traditional classrooms.

Community College Programs

You should determine your long-range goals when you choose your career so that you are aware of the levels of education you should attain for positions with increasing responsibilities. With greater numbers of adults going on to college to earn degrees, you should think seriously about attending at least a two-year institution for post high school education. Employers are beginning to seek college graduates to fill jobs.

Since the early 1960s, two-year community colleges have expanded educational opportunities to provide the professions, business, and industry with qualified personnel.

Practically all these institutions offer secretarial programs, even if designated by another name, for which an Associate in Applied Science (A.A.S.) degree can be earned. One such program for students that prepares them for secretarial/administrative assistant positions is given in the Secretarial and Office Information Systems program of the Business Department at Bronx Community College of The City University of New York. It is shown below in detail so that you can see, if passed successfully, that students have the qualifications that will enable them to handle jobs with increasing responsibilities that were formerly done by managers.

DEPARTMENT OF BUSINESS SECRETARIAL STUDIES CURRICULUM
60 CREDITS REQUIRED FOR A.A.S. DEGREE

First Semester

Fundamentals of Written Composition I
History of the Modern World
Keyboarding I
Business Mathematics or Introduction to Internet and
    Web Development
Fundamentals of Interpersonal Communication
Physical Education—activity course

Second Semester

Keyboarding II
Machine Transcription I
Information Processing Applications and Administration
Introduction to Business or Fundamental Accounting I
Introduction to Mathematical Thought

Third Semester

Keyboarding III
Machine Transcription II
Introduction to Office Automation Concepts or Multimedia
    Theory and Applications for Business
Information Processing Office Simulation
Science Course

Free Elective
Senior Orientation

Fourth Semester

Supervision and Administration of Office Automation
Business Communications
Office Procedures
Introduction to Desktop Publishing
Psychology or Sociology or Public Speaking and Critical Listening
Art Survey or Music Survey

An Associate of Science degree program in Computer Information Technology is offered at Draughons Junior College, an accredited independent college in Nashville, Tennessee. This curriculum will prepare students with the skills and knowledge necessary for a position as an office assistant and computer information technician. In addition to the general education and specialized courses such as microcomputing, office procedures, computer programs, and desktop publishing, students also take Option 1, Emphasis on Information Processing. This enhances their knowledge of software programs, operating systems, accounting, and database. The curriculum requirements are shown below.

DRAUGHONS JUNIOR COLLEGE
COMPUTER INFORMATION TECHNOLOGY DEGREE
62 SEMESTER HOURS

General Education Requirements

English Composition I
English Composition II
General Psychology
Fundamentals of Speech
College Mathematics
U.S. History Since 1877

Major Program Requirements

Career Development
Keyboarding I
Keyboarding II
Introduction to Microcomputing

Business Math
Principles of Accounting I
Business Communications
Records Management
Office Procedures
WordPerfect for Windows
Excel for Windows
MicroSoft Word for Windows
MicroSoft Office
Desktop Publishing Concepts and Applications

Emphasis on Information Processing

Lotus for Windows
WordPerfect/DOS
Fourth Generation Language Applications—Access
Computer Operating Systems and Hardware
Microcomputer Accounting

A rather unique Associate of Arts Degree in Business, a two-year program, was developed at Indiana University of Pennsylvania, which is part of Pennsylvania's State System of Higher Education to confer doctoral degrees. The objectives in designing such a program were to provide business occupational education with the opportunity for specialization in computer and office information systems, to enable students to accept positions in this field, to upgrade knowledge and skills, and to provide the foundation for continuance in a four-year degree program. The A.A. program consists of the following courses:

INDIANA UNIVERSITY OF PENNSYLVANIA
ASSOCIATE OF ARTS—BUSINESS

Major Business (Associate) Core Required Courses

Introduction to Business
Business Technical Writing
Accounting Principles I
Accounting Principles II
Foundations of Business Mathematics
Keyboarding and Document Formatting
Electronic Office Procedures

Introduction to Business Law
Essentials of Finance
Introduction to Management Information Systems
Introduction to Microcomputers

Other Requirements—Computer and Office Specialization

Word Processing Applications
Business Systems Analysis and Design
Business Applications in COBOL
Business Computer Application Project

Specialized Secretarial Areas

An A.A.S. degree can be earned in the specialized secretarial fields, too; however, you must research the college catalogs to find out which two-year institutions have programs for legal, medical, educational, or technical secretaries. You may also check the catalogs of colleges that offer both an Associate in Science degree (A.S.) as well as a four-year Bachelor of Science degree (B.S.).

Legal Specialty

A specialized curriculum option for legal careers is offered in the Office Technology-Legal department at Nassau Community College in Garden City, New York. Skills and knowledge related to a law office that students in the program learn are speedwriting, machine transcription of legal documents, administrative management principles, and legal office procedures. The legal curriculum is illustrated below.

NASSAU COMMUNITY COLLEGE
OFFICE TECHNOLOGY-LEGAL
A.A.S. PROGRAM

First Semester

College Keyboarding I
Word Processing Applications I
Speedwriting I
Administrative Management
Composition I
Activity Course(s)

Second Semester

Speedwriting II
Word Processing Applications II
Legal Office Procedures I
Business Writing
Elective
Activity Course(s)

Third Semester

Shorthand Transcription I or Machine Transcription I
Legal Office Procedures II
Legal Workshop
Health Elective
Mathematics Elective
Social Science Elective

Fourth Semester

Legal Work/Study
Office Technology Elective
Humanities Elective
Social Science Elective
Lab Science Elective

Medical Specialty

A medical curriculum in the Secretarial/Office Information Systems program of the Business Department is offered at Bronx Community College of the City University of New York. These students may work in a variety of physicians' offices, hospitals, clinics, and laboratories. Students learn to transcribe medical documents from recorded dictation, complete medical forms, maintain office records, and manage a medical office. They learn how to use several software programs and become familiar with medical terminology and clinical techniques. Emphasis is also placed on secretarial, communications, and human relations skills, as recommended by the American Association of Medical Assistants. The curriculum follows:

DEPARTMENT OF BUSINESS
SECRETARIAL SCIENCE—MEDICAL CURRICULUM
60 CREDITS REQUIRED FOR A.A.S. DEGREE

First Semester

Fundamentals of Written Composition I
Human Biology
History of the Modern World
Keyboarding I
Business Mathematics

Second Semester

Keyboarding II
Machine Transcription I
Information Processing Application and Administration
Introduction to Business
Medical Terminology
Introduction to Mathematical Thought

Third Semester

Keyboarding III
Clinical Techniques I
Critical Issues in Health
Fundamentals of Interpersonal Communication
Psychology
Introduction to Art or Introduction to Music

Fourth Semester

Business Communications
Medical Office Procedures and Management
Information Processing Office Simulation
Clinical Techniques II
Medical Law
Physical Education—activity course
Senior Orientation

Word Processing

With the explosion of office technology, information systems, and more specifically word processing, many colleges have developed programs for students who are interested in secretarial careers in word processing environments. Concepts, theory, and equipment training are being taught in a variety of ways. The Office Technology Department at Nassau Community College has a curriculum designated as Office Technology, Word Processing, and Office Automation. Below is a copy of the required courses.

NASSAU COMMUNITY COLLEGE
OFFICE TECHNOLOGY, WORD PROCESSING, AND OFFICE AUTOMATION
A.A.S. PROGRAM

First Semester

College Keyboarding I
Word Processing Applications I
Speedwriting I
Administrative Management
Composition I
Activity Course(s)

Second Semester

Word Processing Applications II
Speedwriting II
Business Writing
Elective
Social Science Electives
Activity Course(s)

Third Semester

Machine Transcription I
Executive Workshop
Word Processing Applications III
Math Elective
Health Elective
Social Science Electives

Fourth Semester

Desktop Publishing
Executive Work/Study
Office Technology Elective
Laboratory Science Elective
Humanities Electives

For students who wish to enroll in a one-year program only, particularly adults who either wish to reenter the labor market or update their skills, several institutions have developed certificate programs in word processing. These curricula provide training in procedures, concepts, and electronic equipment needed for positions in organizations that use word processing and information systems. Machine transcription skills and reinforcement of English skills—spelling, grammar, punctuation, and vocabulary—also receive emphasis. Nassau Community College in Garden City, New York, also offers such a program.

The Office Technology Department also offers the ENCORE program, which consists of a sequence of courses that is designed for mature students who want to upgrade their office skills. Students earn fifteen credits that may be applied toward another program in the department.

Private Colleges and Business Schools

In addition to the public community colleges, private two-year colleges as well as private business schools offer one- and two-year secretarial programs. You may wish to check on the accreditation of these schools before enrolling. Private business schools are also a primary source for business training. In many of them, students may enroll at any time, not necessarily at the beginning of the term, and may progress at their own rate.

Continuing Education Programs

In addition to the schools already mentioned, secretarial courses are offered in almost all continuing education programs—in colleges, in evening high schools, at the YMCAs, and wherever self-development is a major objective.

Internships

Other learning experiences are through internship programs or cooperative work experience. This experience helps bridge the gap between college and the real world. Generally, classroom study is combined with supervised on-the-job work. Students may be placed in internships for one semester, but they also attend weekly seminars at the college with sharing of job experiences and features of the work environment. In cooperative work experience programs, arrangements vary. Sometimes students work part-time while attending college, or they may work for a certain block of time and then return to the college. The coordinator usually identifies job openings, arranges interviews, and supervises students. Well-run programs match student skills and interests to employer needs.

Company-Sponsored Programs

Company-sponsored programs are also conducted to provide opportunities for additional learning or reinforcement of skills that are relevant to company activities. Frequently, when a considerable number of employees are deficient in certain kinds of knowledge or skills, as perceived by supervisors or by employees themselves, courses are designed to meet these needs.

Once you are established in a job and sense new needs that are shared by others in your department or skill area, it is sometimes possible to initiate training programs in your company. If you have a good idea that would benefit the company as well as the workers, write a brief proposal and talk it over with your immediate superior. Give that person a chance to discuss it with the personnel department or with her or his supervisor. It is much more likely to receive a favorable response if you follow channels and are polite and businesslike about making the proposal. Some examples of times that such a proposal might be appropriate are when the company would benefit from using new types of equipment such as computers or printers. Keep in mind that the important factor is whether or not the company will be benefited by the proposed training program. More information on company training programs is given in Chapter 8.

SECRETARIAL PROGRAMS IN CANADA

The nature and level of skills required in the labor market has changed in Canada, as in the United States. In the office, it is commonplace to use computer technology for word processing, spreadsheets, database management, desktop publishing, and information storage. Secretaries need to have excellent keyboarding, communications, English, organizational, and analytical skills. The technological innovations have changed the way work is done, who does it, and the skills required. To prepare youth for employment, the government's long-term goal is "to make cooperative education programs available in every high school in Canada."

In Canada, secretarial jobs are the largest group of information-based jobs in the economy. If employed in a specialized area such as medicine, law, or commerce, it is necessary to understand the technical language. Similar to the United States, the basic requirement for entry-level secretarial positions is high school graduation. Some employers are looking for individuals who have earned a secretarial career certificate or have completed a college-level office program. The demand is growing for individuals with college education. Those graduates from related fields of business, commerce, management, and administration, including university graduates, compete for secretarial jobs when they cannot find employment in their field of study.

Some of the programs offered at the Open Learning Agency and most colleges are secretarial, word processing, computer application, legal, and medical secretarial preparation. For those interested in supervisory and administrative positions, administrative programs are available. The prerequisites for admission into the secretarial career field in the community colleges vary from institution to institution. Generally, candidates must pass an English proficiency test and must have completed advanced English courses at the high school level, must meet established typing and shorthand standards, and frequently are required to pass an interview. The two-year program is offered in all community colleges in all of the provinces, with the exception of one or two depending on the course of study.

Statistics show that in 1994, 2,740 students graduated from the two-year community college secretarial career program. According to *Job Futures, Occupational Outlooks,* a government publication, in the Secretarial-General program, the majority found work as secretaries, and the others in clerical occupations. Six out of seven graduates found full-time employment. However, there didn't appear to be much mobility in the secretarial position. In contrast, there was greater mobility among clerical employees who, after three to five years, were employed as secretaries.

Secretaries, recorders, and transcriptionists work in government and throughout the private sector including law offices, company legal departments, real estate companies, land titles offices, courts, doctors' offices, hospitals, clinics, and other medical organizations. This occupational group also includes executive, private, and technical secretaries; estate, medical, legal, litigation, and real estate secretaries; court reporters; and stenographers. There were 421,000 workers employed in this group in 1994, which was 3 percent of the total workforce. In this group, 80 percent were secretaries. The number of women employed in these occupations ranged from 92 percent to 100 percent. Most of the employees in these occupations were 99 percent women.

The *Annual Report on Employment Equity,* which covers the fiscal year from April 1, 1996, to March 31, 1997, reveals that approximately one-half of the federal public service workforce were women, 49.5 percent; almost a quarter of all employees in the executive category were women, 23 percent; just over seven out of ten women entered the federal public service via the administrative support category; and women continued to receive more than half of all promotions, 56.5 percent.

The speed at which technology is moving and the impact it has on the office environment and office occupations stresses the importance of lifetime learning.

CHAPTER 8

PROMOTIONAL OPPORTUNITIES FOR SECRETARIAL PERSONNEL

"Corporations that downsized, de-layered, and re-engineered themselves...have found they cannot run their businesses with a few executives at the top, the worker bees at the bottom, and nobody in between," according to the *Washington Post,* Monday, April 13, 1998. The middle layers of business must now be rebuilt. This is an opportune time for today's secretaries and administrative professionals—who have acquired many managerial skills and knowledge after assuming responsibilities formerly held by managers before downsizing and middle management layoffs began—to be promoted into these middle levels—managerial and professional. Statistics show that the percentage of managers in the workforce is on the rise. However, the work they perform is of a different nature from what their counterparts did a decade ago. No longer will they transmit the boss's order; they will act as a coach, team leader, handholder, and overseer of projects. The *Star Ledger* stated that opportunities that will provide potential career paths available to secretaries and administrative support professionals are related to desktop publishing, the Internet, and customer service support functions of organizations.

About half of today's working women are college educated. Those in secretarial positions aren't satisfied remaining at lower-level jobs. They seek advancement into supervisory and managerial positions. Four factors over the next few decades that portend better opportunities for women are:

1. Approximately one-half of the workforce will be comprised of women.
2. The number of qualified males in the workforce is shrinking.

3. Management style in forward-looking corporations is changing from a hierarchal mode to one with employee involvement.
4. Women are more comfortable working in a participatory management environment than are their male counterparts.

Secretaries who perceive themselves as professionals are career-oriented individuals who have set specific goals for themselves. They do not perceive their position as a dead-end job. Rather, in their pursuit of achieving designated targets, they direct all activities, both in and out of the office, toward this effort. They continually strive to strengthen their personal and professional qualifications. These individuals differ from secretaries who are content to remain in their own little niche, performing the tasks typically assigned to them, no more and no less. Career-oriented individuals are intellectually active, innovative, and willing to do more than is required. They frequently strive for accreditation to improve in their profession and constantly seek ways to better themselves.

Advancement happens when persons plan strategies that include the following: maximizing of all work experiences, enrollment in continuing education courses, participation in workshops and seminars, extensive reading of professional literature, memberships in professional and community organizations, leadership roles in associations, awareness of societal needs, and knowledge of economic trends.

Generally, supervisory and managerial personnel advanced to their promotion in one or more steps. Becoming a supervisor of secretaries and/or other office personnel is the first step in the career ladder that involves planning, organizing, leading, and control. It is a position of responsibility and authority, one that places emphasis on managing human resources. The special skills a supervisor needs to manage others include personal attributes, creativity, an understanding of the factors that affect trends in the labor force, a knowledge and familiarity with changing technology, and the ability to influence workers and to gain their full support in carrying out the goals of the organization.

In this chapter, you will become familiar with the personal qualities and competencies needed for secretarial advancement as well as the paths you can follow to achieve your goals.

PERSONAL QUALITIES

Secretaries work in varied environments, probably no two exactly alike. They perform a multitude of tasks, some requiring much decision making.

Office automation has reduced the static nature of some secretarial jobs and has converted them into dynamic careers with unlimited promotional opportunities for forward-looking, ambitious, qualified individuals. In these environments, higher-level personal qualities are required for success and advancement. Within the context of the definitions of a secretary, as developed by the Professional Secretaries International and as used by the Bureau of Labor Statistics, specific personal traits are desirable: namely, the exercise of initiative and judgment; the ability to interpret requests; the implementation of action-decisions; the ability to interact with executives, managers, staff, clients, and suppliers; and the capability of working independently. These characteristics indicate that a secretary is a highly qualified person who possesses not only a mastery of office skills but also personality requisites of the highest order. A further look at the help-wanted ads supports this concept of higher-order traits. Some frequently used adjectives and phrases to describe the kind of secretary needed are: articulate, personable, self-confident, dynamic, bright, hard-working, unflappable in deadline-paced office, and flexible team worker. The secretary who possesses the qualities just enumerated usually gets ahead and eventually occupies a position of influence and status.

Surveyed employers are looking for candidates who are mature and don't have a know-it-all attitude, are aggressive and not pushy, have self-confidence and are not arrogant. The ten personal characteristics employers want candidates to possess are listed in Table 18.[1]

These same employers are also looking for well-rounded employees who have good interpersonal skills, can act efficiently and effectively in the workplace, and can ask pertinent questions. Other skills employers want are ranked on a scale of one to five, with five being considered extremely important. See Table 19.

In addition to what employers are looking for, employees must be able to derive satisfaction from the job. The variety and level of tasks

---

[1]Claudia Allen, "The Job Outlook for '98 Grads," *Journal of Career Planning and Employment,* National Association of Colleges and Employees (Winter 1998).

Table 18. TOP 10 PERSONAL CHARACTERISTICS EMPLOYERS SEEK IN JOB CANDIDATES

1. honesty/integrity
2. motivation/initiative
3. communication skills
4. self-confidence
5. flexibility
6. interpersonal skills
7. strong work ethic
8. teamwork skills
9. leadership skills
10. enthusiasm

performed by the secretary/office professional directly influence job satisfaction, a human need that motivates individuals to achieve to the maximum of their abilities. Job satisfaction usually means happiness with the job, therefore, a more pleasing personality.

Table 19. SKILLS EMPLOYERS WANT

5-point scale; 5=extremely important

4.67	interpersonal
4.65	teamwork
4.56	analytical
4.53	oral communication
4.52	flexibility
4.32	computer
4.12	written communications
4.08	leadership
4.05	work experience
3.77	internship experience
3.37	co-op experience

A study by Steelcase, Inc., revealed that the prestigious corner office is no longer desirable. Only 17 percent of American office workers would choose it. Almost a majority of the respondents indicated they spend eight hours or more daily at their work space and are more interested in comfort and control over that space. More storage accounted for 27 percent of the responses; better technology support, 18 percent; more privacy, 18 percent; more comfortable chair, 17 percent; better lighting, 14 percent; more tackable space, 11 percent; and more space for impromptu meetings, 10 percent.

One thousand employees were asked to rank ten possible motivational rewards. The same test was then given to the employers. Notice the difference in ranking. The employees ranked "interesting work" as the first element of importance with "full appreciation of work" second and "a feeling of being in on things" third. The supervisors rate the same elements much lower in value. In effect, the secretary really wants recognition and appreciation for the job being done. See the charts ranking motivational rewards below:[2]

What's important to employees?	*What do supervisors think is important to employees?*
• interesting work	• good wages
• full appreciation of work done	• job security
• a feeling of being in on things	• promotion and growth in organization
• job security	• good working conditions
• good wages	• interesting work
• promotion and growth in organization	• personal loyalty to employees
• good working conditions	• tactful discipline
• personal loyalty to employees	• full appreciation of work done
• tactful discipline	• sympathetic help with personal problems
• sympathetic help with personal problems	• a feeling of being in on things

Research tells us that one of the most important competencies for a secretary is the ability to maintain good human relations. Personnel who have pleasing personalities, are courteous, and are cooperative usually function more successfully in the open plan office designs where there is greater

---

[2]"Differing Views on Motivation," *The Secretary* (June/July 1996): 5.

interaction among employees. These are also valuable qualities for harmonious working relationships in team projects. Frequently, when considering job mobility, many employers rank personal traits, congeniality, dependability, dedication, discretion, and self-assertiveness as important as skills and knowledge.

SKILLS

An important part of exploring secretarial careers is to investigate the functions of positions and the concomitant skills and knowledge needed to fulfill the duties and responsibilities of the job. Also, be certain to identify the higher-level skills of supervisors and managers. This information can then be used to determine how you will develop those skills in which you are deficient. The individual who merely performs routine tasks that anyone with minimal skills can do is easily replaceable.

In numerous articles that appeared in *The Secretary,* the following traits were primarily those that contribute most to success on the job and to upward mobility to managerial positions:

- computer technology skills
- proficiency in latest software programs
- expert problem-solving skills
- high-level decision-making abilities
- personnel management skills
- project management abilities
- budget management abilities
- human relations skills
- public speaking skills and writing skills
- crisis management skills
- organizational skills
- language skills

To be considered an outstanding employee, you need to develop all of the above skills, accept challenges, have a positive attitude in life and work, assess your strengths and weaknesses, and continue learning by attending conventions, seminars, and workshops. Believe in yourself and strive to reach your goals.

To get ahead in the secretarial profession, individuals who have broad skills and knowledge in information processing and who have the necessary administrative ability will be most likely to reach higher levels of responsibility in either supervisory or managerial positions.

PATHS TO PROFESSIONAL GROWTH

Professional growth is the key to career satisfaction. As you become involved in activities that lead to self-improvement, you become not only more valuable to your employer but a potential candidate for promotion. To realize your maximum level of abilities, you should avail yourself of every opportunity that will further develop you personally as well as your skills and knowledge. Below are some suggestions for growing professionally:

1. Join professional organizations whose membership consists of supervisory and managerial personnel, or some other business-related group such as data processing. This will be a broadening experience because of the contacts you make in fields of business other than secretarial. During organizational meetings or seminars, you will have opportunities to share ideas with other interested members.

2. Become involved in organizational projects that develop leadership skills.

3. Volunteer your services in your area of expertise.

4. Assume jobs that will give you a high visibility.

5. Find a mentor, a high-level manager or executive who can advise and guide you. In reaching your goals, this person may also recommend you to the "right" contacts.

6. Listen attentively to what others are saying.

7. Become a specialist in a particular area, such as personnel evaluation.

8. Visit equipment exhibitors and attend seminars.

9. Read professional literature, such as *Working Woman, The Secretary, Today's Office,* and *Datamation.*

10. Seek accreditation in a profession other than secretarial, such as Certified Administrative Manager (CAM).

PROFESSIONAL ORGANIZATIONS

Through memberships in organizations, you make important contacts. Companies frequently pay membership dues for employees who join professional organizations and reimburse them for costs incurred when attending meetings and conferences. Both company and employee benefit—the worker in terms of personal and professional growth, the company in terms of visibility and contribution to the educational process.

As an active member, you meet other individuals with similar or related interests. You also have opportunities to develop your communication and leadership skills by joining committees formed for specific tasks. From presenters at meetings who share some of their expertise with you, you broaden your horizons and learn a great deal.

You should join organizations other than secretarial for broadening experiences. You will not only add to your knowledge base but will also begin to gain visibility in the business community. From participation in seminars and conventions, you will also gain many ideas which in turn will help you become more creative. Your association with other professionals will enhance your professional growth in terms of knowledge, understanding of trends in business, and managerial concepts.

In Chapter 5, you learned about the International Association of Administrative Professionals, formerly known as Professional Secretaries International, and its certifying program, as well as about the specialized secretarial organizations, their activities and purposes. A few other professional associations that provide good opportunities for making contacts and growing professionally are as follows:

- National Association of Legal Secretaries (NALS), a professional association for all legal support staff. It has 250 chapters nationwide and sponsors certification programs.
- Association of Information Systems Professionals (AISP), an information management organization with local chapters throughout the United States. It sponsors an annual symposium and publishes valuable literature.
- Administrative Management Society (AMS), with more than 140 chapters throughout the United States and Canada and dedicated to promoting the professional goals of persons in management. A

valuable project it sponsors is the certification program for the manager, known as Certified Administrative Manager (CAM).
- Data Processing Management Association (DPMA).
- The Association of Records Managers and Administrators (ARMA).

All of these organizations have local chapters that you ought to investigate for membership.

COMPANY TRAINING PROGRAMS

Society will continue to experience greater changes during this decade than it has in the past. New job categories will emerge, job requirements will change, the way in which work is performed will vary, and where work is done will change. Companies are beginning to realize that people have become the major asset of a business enterprise; therefore, training is a critical element in a firm's operations.

As automated systems are updated, it is necessary to train employees to operate the sophisticated equipment and to learn the new procedures. Educational training programs are not new in corporate training departments. Through the years, trainers have been designing and scheduling courses offered either during company hours or after working hours. Generally, these programs are established to:

- orient employees to company procedures
- train employees on new equipment
- provide opportunities for additional learning relevant to company activities
- provide employees with job enrichment as well as new jobs and responsibilities
- develop basic and advanced skills in areas such as English, writing, and software programs
- provide remediation for those who demonstrate a need
- learn new skills and knowledge for upward mobility
- prepare for career switching

Many companies offer structured training in the form of in-service programs, which consist of three basic types:

1. *On-the-job training,* in which beginning workers are trained at their workstations under the supervision of an experienced worker.
2. *Vestibule training* (usually conducted by larger firms), in which training is given away from the work area but usually during working hours. Instruction is provided with generally the same equipment, materials, and procedures as pertain to the actual job in an on-site classroom. The objectives of this training are to raise levels of employees' skills, to orient them to company procedures, and to teach advanced skills for promotional opportunities.
3. *After-hours* or *off-premises training,* which is taken voluntarily by employees for personal development.

TUITION-REIMBURSEMENT PROGRAMS

Many companies with training plans allow employees to enroll in college or university courses. For example, in tuition-refund plans, personnel enroll in undergraduate or graduate courses in local colleges or in continuing education classes, which have been one of the fastest-growing educational areas. The adult segment of the population usually registers in continuing education courses to update skills, as a refresher, or for professional development.

Payment for education outside company programs falls under two general categories: partial or full reimbursement. Policies vary greatly from firm to firm, some requiring that the course be job-related and others that a grade of C or better be earned. Some companies reimburse employees based on actual grade received; others pay a stipulated amount for a course at a college and a lesser sum for a course at a nonaccredited institution or professional school. Still other institutions share the tuition and registration expenses. Many companies, however, do reimburse employees for total course expenditures if completed successfully.

The bottom line of continuing education is professional growth with the potential for upward mobility. Company training programs are usually beneficial to both employee and employer in terms of productivity, loyalty, skills, and knowledge.

NETWORK

Traditionally, men automatically formed groups for the purpose of support and sharing information. Today, women are forming networks to combat isolation and to learn more about business tactics. Career women organize to get ahead in the business world by networking. They share ideas, exchange career information, and receive moral support in the pursuit of their careers. Women have formed special groups for the purpose of helping one another gain self-confidence, become assertive, acquire knowledge, earn more money, and develop clout. Members are linked as part of a communications network. In such a group, you gain the emotional support to pursue your goals. You also become more visible in the business community, sharing personal experiences with others. You realize that you are not alone. In effect, the network is the vehicle through which you will be exposed to contacts and information that will help you grow. Building personal and professional relationships is important. Don't let friends fade away. Instead, reestablish old friendships by making a phone call.

When you network, you are developing contacts with individuals who might be helpful in your career. There are numerous ways in all industries for employees to become acquainted. They may know of potential openings or may know of somebody else to whom they can introduce you. Research indicates that leads are one of the most effective ways of finding out about a job. In addition to being helpful in your job search, these individuals can lend emotional support. To benefit from such a group, you should abide by the following principles and strategies:

- Join and become active in a professional association.
- Become involved with a civic, social, or religious organization.
- Keep organized records of contacts—names, addresses, and telephone numbers.
- Be a good listener, ask questions, and show interest.
- Give as well as receive information.
- Lend someone a helping hand.
- Make a point of talking to your supervisors and coworkers on a regular basis if you are a telecommuter.

- Build confidence by assessing your strengths.
- Show respect to others.
- Be aware of what is happening in your firm and in the field.

Networking, according to the literature, should help you believe in yourself, which is the first step toward success. This technique has been adopted by numerous women in many occupations all over the country. Make certain that your contact network grows and does not shrink. Be optimistic, pleasant, and lively when with other people. These characteristics are attractive to others and help build relationships.

CHAPTER 9

THE JOB SEARCH IN THE INFORMATION AGE—UNITED STATES AND CANADA

"It's not the best prepared student who gets the job, but the student who is best prepared at getting the job," is a statement that gets right to the point when looking for employment. There are many ways in which to hunt for a job; however, initially you should do some research on the workplace to gain some understanding of the latest trends both in the office environment and competition in the workforce. The traditional sources used and the electronic method of going on-line to find a job will be discussed later in this chapter.

You have read in this book about many options within the secretarial field. As you begin to search for employment, you will find that you have many decisions to make as to the kind of firm you would like to work for, where you would like to live, whether you work better on your own or as part of a group, whether a particular industry or profession is more compatible with your interests and abilities, whether you prefer a large automated office or a small traditional-type environment. The first job you accept has a very important influence on you. This is your first work experience in your chosen profession, and it shapes your attitudes about the career.

The career you choose should unlock your potential for achievement on the job and bring about personal growth. This can only occur when your goals, skills, knowledge, and ambitions are matched to the job you select. You should take a personal inventory to determine your interests, strengths, and weaknesses. These factors should be considered in the selection of a job that will enable you to progress into more responsible positions. Above all, choose a job where the atmosphere and pace are comfortable for you and where the job responsibilities are compatible with your abilities.

This chapter will prepare you to make decisions about your initial position and plan your strategies for your job search.

LOCATION

With the growing number of professional centers and business complexes being constructed in the suburbs, secretaries do have choices of either working close to home or traveling. Generally, salaries are higher in the cities than in the suburban districts; however, depending on your values and needs, each location has particular advantages.

Main offices of banks, stores, and government agencies, as well as executive offices and showrooms of large corporations, are usually found in the cities. In these metropolitan areas, employees have the benefit of theater and shopping that usually are not duplicated in outlying districts. The atmosphere is usually more sophisticated; there is greater emphasis on dress code; and more money is spent on food, entertainment, and clothing. In suburban districts, dress is more casual and living expenses are lower.

You have to search your inner feelings to determine whether you enjoy crowds, usually a part of city life, and the hub of activity rather than the landscaped areas and quiet surroundings usually found in rural towns.

TYPE AND SIZE OF OFFICE

If you have special interests in music, art, or medicine, which for various reasons you could not pursue as a career field, you might wish to find a job in an industry related to them. For example, an individual who is interested in music might secure employment with a publisher of musical scores; in art, with a museum; and in medicine, with a hospital or clinic. Keep in mind that the most satisfying career for you will be the one that is in harmony with your interests.

In a small office, you will have opportunities to perform a multitude of tasks. However, no matter how skillfully you perform your duties, there is very little room for advancement. Jobs are available in offices of private doctors, dental offices, real estate offices, branch offices of banks, insurance companies, lawyers, and engineers. The atmosphere is usually less rigid and more informal than in the large office where large numbers of personnel are employed and accountable. Although working hours are regulated, the secretary does have more freedom to change work schedules. Depending on where you work, bus service may or may not be available; however, employees usually drive to work where parking space is provided. A disadvantage is that salaries are more related to a company's fixed budget rather than your competence.

In large offices, the environment is more structured, lines of authority are clearly defined, and personnel policies are set. Because of departmental structure, work is specialized. In a more or less traditional setting, the executive secretary who works on a one-to-one basis for the president or another major executive may handle the administrative details of mail, e-mail, faxing, record keeping, appointments, correspondence, and meetings. In an automated environment that is fully equipped with the latest office technology and systems, the secretary/administrative assistant/ office professional usually supports several managers in the organization and has a very wide range of responsibilities, including managerial and administrative duties. This employee generally has good technical skills, both oral and written communication skills, and a personality and personal attributes that make a good team player. No matter in which size office you prefer being employed, remember that you must always be ready to learn and to remain in a learning mode, for changes continue to occur very quickly. The skills you have today might be outmoded in a few months, and so will the job change.

Opportunities for advancement to supervisory and managerial positions exist as well as horizontal movement to positions in other departments. Other advantages of working for a large firm are the fringe benefits, which include company training programs and tuition-reimbursement plans, company-subsidized cafeterias, bonuses, scholarships for children of employees, day-care centers, credit unions, stock-buying privileges, group life insurance, medical benefits, hospitalization, and dental insurance. Frequently, the spouse and children under nineteen years of age who are living at home are included in medical insurance plans. These fringe benefits account for approximately 40 percent of company personnel expenses, not including payment of salaries.

CONDUCTING THE JOB SEARCH

After you have identified the secretarial career that you wish to pursue and for which you feel most qualified, determine the geographic area where you would like to work. Then identify companies where you would like to work and where you anticipate openings will occur from downsizing in middle management, growth, or turnover and replacement. If you are uncertain as to where to concentrate your efforts, try to find data on industries that have the best overall employment prospects.

Plan your job search strategies according to the following steps:

- Develop a network of personal contacts.
- Compile a list of target companies and do some research to find out about the companys' products or services, status in the industry, size, growth potential, information about the job of your interest, and person empowered to hire you. Call each company for an annual report and available literature on the firm.
- Use electronic resources and go on the Internet for your search. There are thousands of job listings on the Internet. The World Wide Web is a good area for it has many electronic career centers that offer information of all types, including job listings.
- Develop your resume.
- Write a letter of application.
- Strengthen your interviewing skills and maintain records of interviews.
- Send thank-you letters.

Although the most recent method of searching for a job is on the Internet, continue to use the traditional way to find a job, too—your newspapers and journals, contacts, and agencies. Most important, you must develop a job prospect list. This list should include friends, relatives, instructors, employers, key people in organizations, school placement offices, newspaper advertisements, employment agencies, company recruiters, and company personnel offices.

Friends, Relatives, and Instructors

Let your friends and relatives know that you are seeking a position. Discuss your goals with them and ask them to let you know if a position becomes available in their company or elsewhere. You might ask them to call other acquaintances who might know of openings.

School Placement Offices

Both high school and college placement offices receive calls from businesses indicating job openings. They also have counselors available to advise students. They are experienced in helping you prepare a resume and telling you about part-time and summer employment in addition to full-time work. They may also be able to make good suggestions for interviewing, particularly if they know something about the firm.

It is advisable to file a portfolio with the placement office. It should contain recommendations from teachers, a personal data sheet, and other credentials. Keep this information current so that your employment status is up to date. Executive recruiters who come to the colleges to interview students examine this portfolio.

Advertisements in Newspapers and Professional Magazines

Read these ads regularly. From them you will soon learn what kinds of employees are needed, where openings are available, and what skills are needed. You will also gain insight into salaries offered, and even benefits. These advertisements have either a company name and address or are "blind" whereby you respond to a box number or a telephone number. Blind ads are placed to eliminate unqualified applicants.

Answer an ad promptly with a letter of application and a resume. Read carefully for aspects of the job mentioned, such as "savvy and poise," "high voltage person with grasp of detail," "ambitious," "highly organized," "good phone personality," "knowledge of Word," and "computer literate." Also check to see if anything in the ad makes this company unique, such as a four-day work week or flexible hours.

Employment Agencies

Employment agencies are of two types: public and private. You may register without a fee at a public employment agency by completing an application form, taking an English test and computer skills test, and being interviewed. Many state agencies are tied into a job-bank program where openings are fed into a computer and where a printout is available to anyone who wants it. The state employment agencies are linked together in a network by the U.S. Employment Service.

Private employment agencies charge a fee, usually paid by the employer. They have many leads to good jobs, but use these firms with caution. The jobs that sound great in the ads aren't always available when you get there. Also, guard against being swayed by them to take a job that may not be exactly the kind you want. Be sure to register with several agencies that serve your field of work. Private agencies service the companies by doing the preliminary screening, testing, and interviewing. Only applicants with the qualifications for the job are sent to the company seeking help. These agencies range in size and some of them cater to certain skill areas or fields of work.

Refer to the section of Temporary Employment in Chapter 4 where outsourcing is discussed. You may sign up with this type of agency, too.

Government Service

There are hundreds of thousands of secretarial openings in civil service each year in cities and towns throughout the nation as well as in foreign countries. All except a few of these jobs require a competitive examination before appointment. Test results are entered on a list in ranked order of scores. Books written specifically for civil service examinations are available in local bookstores and can help you prepare for these tests. To be eligible for appointment, an applicant must be a citizen of the United States and must meet the minimum age, training, and experience requirements for the position.

FedWorld has its own home page on the World Wide Web. Job opening are one of the many information topics from the federal government that you can access. You can connect to FedWorld by modem by keying this address: http://www.fedworld.gov. From the menu, select "Federal Job Openings."

Career Placement Registry, Inc.

Students on many campuses may record their personal and academic credentials in an international direct-access database. Employers are able to access information in these databases.

If you wish to register, you need to complete a special Student Data Entry Form, submit a one-page typed or printed resume, and send it together with a $15 fee to the Career Placement Registry for six months' service on the on-line retrieval database. A printout of the computer record created from the form you complete will be sent to you for verification. For more information, you may write directly to CPR, 3202 Kirkwood Highway, Wilmington, DE 19808.

Job Searching on the Internet

In addition to the number and diversity of jobs you might find on the Internet, and the fact that it is a powerful search tool, there are several other advantages for using it. 1. You may be able to delve into the hidden job market, which is the world of unadvertised openings; 2. Many major corporations list job openings on web sites because employers can fill jobs faster and less expensively; 3. Individuals looking for jobs can can send their resumes to firms either locally or across the country; 4. Job hunters can find a list of jobs organized in many categories, such as state, occupation, industry, or part-time/full-time; 5. A search can be done at any hour of the day and doesn't interfere with a work schedule; 6. Information on the interview process and type of questions asked can be found. The major disadvantage to using the Internet is that the information you send is not private.

Other Sources

The Yellow Pages of the telephone directory can be used to make cold calls to personnel departments or employment offices. You may also write a letter of application to companies for which you would like to work. You may enclose a resume with this letter and indicate you will call to determine if a position is available. This call or correspondence might reach the company at an opportune time for you, perhaps the very day when an employee makes known his or her resignation. The job applicant who uses this technique is looked upon as someone with initiative and aggressiveness.

You may also apply directly to a business by walking into a personnel department and filing an application. If there are no openings at the time, your credentials will be filed for later reference; however, it is wise to follow up with an occasional call.

Contact as many sources as you believe can help. Do not sit back and wait for things to happen. Conduct an active job campaign.

When you look for a job, you really have to sell yourself very much the way you would sell a product. In this instance, you are the product that you want to sell to a firm so that you can be hired for a specific job. To do so effectively, you must know yourself and evaluate yourself honestly. You sell yourself through a resume, an application letter, and an interview. In each of these processes, you should remember to accentuate your strengths. Let the employer know that you are confident in your abilities to assume the responsibilities of the job.

THE APPLICATION LETTER

The application letter is the first step in securing a position, and it is sent usually in response to an advertisement in the help-wanted section of the paper. Generally it is accompanied by a resume. This letter should highlight aspects of your background that support your statement that you are the right person for the job.

This letter is the very first impression you make on the recipient. It should be not only neat and visually attractive but an attention-getter, one that establishes a contact. A letter usually has three parts:

1. *The opening* should create interest, state your purpose, and reveal where you learned of the opening: "If you are seeking a mature, responsible, creative administrative assistant, as advertised in today's *Los Angeles Times,* then I am the person for you."

2. *The body* of the letter should contain convincing statements that show how your qualifications, education, and experience meet the employer's requirements. In this section, express a genuine interest in the company and make a positive statement why you would like to work for them: "I am impressed not only with your

products but also with the many activities you support in this city. Working for your company, I know, would be a valuable learning experience." Or, "My work with the elderly, my background in psychology, and my excellent communication skills make me the very logical candidate for the job."

3. *The closing* paragraph should stimulate action by requesting an interview. Indicate that you will call at a particular time to arrange for this: "I would very much like to be interviewed for the position. I will call your office Thursday morning to speak with you about an appointment. If you wish to reach me before Thursday, my telephone number is (321) 555-0000."

THE TRADITIONAL RESUME

There are two styles of resumes that have been used for many, many years by applicants when trying to get a job and that will continue to be the current format until the electronic resume is accepted and used by the majority of firms. Traditional resumes are written in a style that gets the reader's attention. This is usually achieved by creativity in expression and use of action verbs, bolding, underlining, bullets, and colored paper. One type is the reverse chronological resume, which lists the dates of employment and educational background in reverse chronological order. The functional format emphasizes skills and accomplishments as they relate to the job for which you are applying. This format stresses your strengths and skill groupings, but it presents your employment history in less detail than does the chronological resume.

A well-prepared resume is a vital tool for individuals seeking employment. It highlights significant details of a person's history and indicates important personal data, career objectives, educational background, work experience, and special interests and accomplishments. A carefully prepared resume should state just enough about your skills and abilities to impress the prospective employer. The time you spend in collecting, analyzing, and preparing the data will serve a two-fold purpose: 1. to sell your qualifications as an employee to an employer, and 2. to prepare you for the interview. Once you have organized the data to reflect your strengths, you can then discuss these items with assurance.

Make your resume unique. You want it to stand out among all those submitted by your competitors. One way to accomplish this is to have it printed on a textured beige or ivory-colored paper. To enhance the appearance of your resume, arrange it skillfully by using wide margins and side headings; keep narrative to one side, properly aligned.

If you are a student with limited work experience, a one-page summary is adequate; however, if you have had extensive experience, advanced education, or significant achievements, then do not hesitate to extend your resume to two pages. Some authorities disagree with this; however, vital data should be included if they reflect strengths and information about you that is relevant to the position you are seeking.

As you begin to accumulate pertinent data, develop an asset list under the headings: personal data, educational background, work experience, special interests and affiliations, and references. After you have gathered these data, discard those items that aren't relevant to secretarial positions and include everything you believe the employer would be interested in knowing about you. A brief description of each section of the resume follows:

Personal Data. Every resume must include the name of the applicant, address, and telephone number. Federal legislation limits inquiries about age, sex, and marital status. However, if you consider these data pertinent to company needs, include them. When making this decision, think it through carefully from an employer's viewpoint. Do not include a photograph or such information as height, weight, race, or religious affiliation.

Career Objective. An effective resume should have a specific career focus. You may indicate the position you would seek after a period of time at this company. Be specific in your statement: "To perform as an administrative assistant to an executive in charge of marketing operations where there are opportunities for professional growth."

Education. If you have a college degree, then it isn't necessary to include high school background. Under this category, include date of graduation, degree or professional certificate earned, major, and courses related to your career choice. Special projects that contributed to your professional development should be included.

In this category, elaborate on the level of skills you have with equipment as well as any language fluency.

Usually special honors, awards, or scholarships are earned during the time you are attending school. These items reflect a good image of you and should become part of your resume.

Work Experience. Undoubtedly, prospective employers will read this section carefully to determine if your past experience relates to the company's needs. Include internships and cooperative work experience programs. Highlight significant data and use action verbs—such as *developed, managed,* and *headed*—to describe the work you have done.

Use reverse chronological order to list your experience; that is, most recent job first. Include title of job and major duties performed.

A few words of caution! Do not leave time gaps under the topic headings in your resume. This keeps an employer guessing and might lead to incorrect assumptions.

Special Interests and Affiliations. Your special interests, hobbies, and extracurricular activities also might give the employer an idea about you. For example, holding an office in a professional organization would show leadership abilities. Involvement in community programs might reflect ability to interact with others.

References. References need not be included on the resume. You may simply state "furnished on request." When you submit names of individuals as references, select those persons who can speak with authority on your performance, such as employers, instructors, and administrators. Do not give the names of friends or relatives. Before you use an individual's name for reference, obtain permission to do so. You might develop a list of names as references so that you can be selective and suggest different people for different positions.

There are several acceptable styles for preparing a resume. You may wish to use the sample resumes in Figure 9.1 and 9.2 as a guide for formatting your own.

THE ON-LINE RESUME

To keep up with the job market, you need to be able to produce an electronic resume that can easily be read and understood by the computer. Electronic resumes must be searchable and scannable by the computer. To be searchable, the applicant developing the resume must use

Figure 9.1 SAMPLE TRADITIONAL RESUME

CECILIA CRUZ
5836 Tulsa Avenue
Milwaukee, WI 53217-0013
(441) 555-9103

CAREER OBJECTIVE	To perform responsibilities of an administrative manager in a secretarial support environment in a legal department
EDUCATION	*Lakeville Community College* A.A.S. Degree 951 Leeds Street Milwaukee, WI 53217-0012
Field of Study	Secretarial and Office Systems, Legal Option
Related Courses	Law Office Management Business Law Introduction to Accounting Legal Procedures Introduction to Psychology
Secretarial Skills	Typewriting, 65 words per minute Shorthand, 120 words per minute Machine Skills: transcriber, personal computer Software Programs: WordPerfect 6.1, Lotus 1-2-3, Word, Excel, Powerpoint
Other Skills	Reading, writing, and conversational fluency in Spanish
Awards and Honors	Certificate for Dean's List earned during Fall, 1996; Spring, 1997; Fall, 1997; and Spring, 1998
WORK EXPERIENCE	
Spring, 1998	Management Internship Training Program Lakeville Community College *Duties:* Assisted secretary to Dean of College. Typed correspondence and reports; handled the telephone
Summer, 1997	Bergman & Wilson Title: Legal Secretary 118-21 Ohio Boulevard Milwaukee, WI 53217-0012 *Duties:* Took dictation in shorthand, answered the telephone, maintained the calendar, transcribed recorded dictation, and inputted legal documents such as wills and agreements on an IBM Pentium II
REFERENCES	Furnished on request

Figure 9.2 SAMPLE FUNCTIONAL RESUME

Maria Marin
15 Robin Street
Worcester, MA 01601-3256
(301) 555-3172

CAREER OBJECTIVE	To perform responsibilities of an administrative manager in a secretarial support environment in a legal department
SPECIAL QUALIFICATIONS	Three years of experience with increasing responsibilities in addition to 30 credits earned toward a B.A. degree in office systems
WORK EXPERIENCE	
Administrative Assistant	Worked for three managers of Warren Industries, Raleigh, North Carolina; set up a filing system for the department; supervised the general clerks; coordinated joint meetings held by senior and junior partners; scheduled appointments with clients
Executive Secretary	Was secretary to one of the vice presidents of a major textile organization; supervised the secretarial staff; performed general administrative assignments; handled confidential files; typed general and legal documents; transcribed legal documents
MEMBERSHIPS	International Association of Administrative Professionals National Association of Legal Secretaries
REFERENCES	Provided upon request

key words or nouns for database searching—not action words. Companies that are advertising job openings through the Internet are beginning to request that resumes are sent through e-mail rather than through the post office or faxed. Recruiters also check on-line resume databases to find candidates for unadvertised job openings. With the right software, employers can now compare hundreds of resumes to compare applicants for the job. However, the New York State Department of Labor acknowledged that "even vast changes need time for their full effects to unfold [referring to electronic resumes]. Right now, the current resume format is not on the brink of extinction, nor has the 'human element' been entirely erased from the job search process."

One of the most popular formats to use when keying an electronic resume for e-mail is the plain text style, which the majority of firms can accept. Use white paper; avoid italics, underlining, different font sizes, graphics, and lines. The computer will read circles as the letter "O"; use solid dots or bullets. To highlight something, use either capital letters, dashes, or asterisks. Another important technique is to make certain a line has no more than sixty-five characters since it cannot be recognized by the computer. Always test the resume for clarity by sending it to yourself before sending it to a company. (See Figure 9.3)

When you post your resume on an on-line database, you are receiving very wide exposure and marketing yourself worldwide. This is a good method to use if you plan to relocate to another city or country.

THE JOB INTERVIEW

The interview is the last and one of the most important steps in being hired for a position. This is your opportunity to sell yourself and to demonstrate that you are the best candidate for the job. This is the first time the employer gets a personal impression of you as an individual and as a prospective employee. Interviews are given in several different ways: telephone, computer, Internet, face-to-face.

The telephone interview has been used in recent years as the first contact an applicant has with a potential employer. The purpose is to get an understanding of the person's background to determine suitability for the job. Either a manager from the firm who has the responsibility of hiring or a human resource person asks the applicant a series of questions on the telephone. If a good impression is made and the candidate has the qualifications, then a date for a face-to-face interview will be set up.

The computerized job interview is now being used by many companies instead of the traditional screening interview. In this situation, the computer asks the questions of the applicants about their background, work experience, and skills. When this system was first developed, the interview consisted of multiple-choice and true/false questions. However, some systems now have questions that require written responses.

Figure 9.3 SAMPLE ELECTRONIC RESUME

```
Cecilia Cruz
5836 Tulsa Avenue
Milwaukee, WI 53217-0013
(441) 555-9103
```

Keywords: Management internship, legal office, Spanish, take dictation in shorthand, assisted secretary to Dean; type, business law, accounting, computer, Dean's list, shorthand, Word Perfect for Windows, 6.1, Lotus 1-2-3, Word, Excel, Powerpoint; telephone, Dean's list

SKILLS

- Typing 65 words per minute
- Shorthand 120 words per minute
- Transcribe recorded dictation
- Key legal documents
- Computer skills
- Use variety of software
- Schedule appointments

EMPLOYMENT HISTORY

Management Internship Training Program at Lakeville Community College, 1998

- Assisted secretary to Dean of College
- Typed correspondence and reports
- Handled the telephone

Legal Secretary, Bergman & Wilson, Summer 1997

- Took dictation in shorthand
- Answered the telephone
- Maintained the calendar
- Inputted legal documents such as wills and agreements

EDUCATION

A.A.S. Degree
Lakeville Community College
Milwaukee, WI

PROFESSIONAL ORGANIZATIONS

National Association of Legal Secretaries
International Association of Administrative Professionals

All questions are customized for relevancy to each company and the position that is open. The interviewer accesses from the computer a summary of the applicant's responses. This might lead to a face-to-face interview. Of interest to you are the special computers with lenses that transmit head-and-shoulder images of the recruiter and interviewee when conducting face-to-face interviews in corporate offices and campus centers.

The Job Internet Interview is used for initial screening. The applicant is given the password to get access to the company's computer system. After logging on, the applicant is asked the usual questions about background, work experience, and skills.

The face-to-face interview conducted in the office environment is the final step to make an impression and to determine if you are interested in the position. Many suggestions are given in the text that follows to prepare you for the interview.

Before the Interview

The interview is a two-way communication process during which unsuitable applicants are screened out. You should plan for this interview so that the experience can be beneficial to you. Some guidelines you might pursue before you go on an interview are: researching the company; evaluating your career goals, values, likes, dislikes, strengths, and weaknesses; dressing appropriately; being yourself; anticipating questions; and preparing supplies.

Researching the company. Before the interview, you should gather as much information as possible about the company, its products and services, its potential for growth, the department and opening for which you are being interviewed, and its reputation in terms of employer-employee relations and community activities. You need to know something about the organization so that you can determine how you can be an asset to the company. In addition, your knowledge about the company and comments reflecting how you can contribute to its operations surely will impress the interviewer.

There are several methods to learn about the company. First, try to get the name and title of the person who will interview you. Then read all you can about the company in the annual reports, in the firm's recruiting brochures, in company publications, and in product news releases. You might call the public relations department of the company and ask for its literature. If you secured this interview from an employment agency, then ask the agency for some insight into the company. Another alternative is to check library reference books and business publications such as *Dun and Bradstreet* reports and *Standard & Poor's*. You might even call a stockbroker. Finally, read the advertisements in the newspapers.

Information on small firms may be gathered from the local chamber of commerce.

Self-evaluation. You should take stock of yourself, what you want in a career, your motivation to achieve, what you have accomplished in previous jobs that demonstrates marketable skills and productivity. Think about your likes and dislikes, and whether your interests match your skills and abilities. Finding out about yourself will help you recognize your own potential. This will enable you to speak with self-confidence about yourself, your interests, and what you have to offer.

Dressing appropriately. Dress conservatively on the day of the interview. Women should avoid excessive jewelry and makeup. Avoid extreme hairstyles. A skirt and blouse, tailored dress, or suit are appropriate. Men should be clean-shaven and dressed in business attire. Jeans will not make a good impression.

Being yourself. You need to be happy working for a company; and, therefore, you ought to be accepted as you really are. However, sometimes it is necessary to modify behavior. For example, you must be friendly, casual, courteous, and professional. Most important, be honest. Remember, the requirements of the job should be matched with a person's talents, desires, and abilities so that both company and employee benefit. The key to a successful interview lies in your ability to convey a positive attitude about yourself.

Anticipating questions. If you anticipate some questions that the interviewer might ask and think about your responses, you might relieve some of your tensions. The interviewer generally is trying to determine self-confidence of applicant, whether career goals are defined, and the interest and enthusiasm that is demonstrated for the position. Other critical behaviors being evaluated are the maturity of individual, self-assertiveness, intelligence, and results orientation.

Questions may be either open-ended or structured, in which specific information is sought. "Ice-breakers" or questions that tend to put the interviewee at ease are generally items that have already been determined during your self-assessment. Typical questions asked during interviews are:

- What can you tell me about your personal background?
- How would you describe yourself?
- Why did you select a secretarial career?
- What do you see yourself doing five years from now?
- What approaches are you going to use to reach your ultimate career goals?
- What are some of your major strengths?
- What are your biggest weaknesses? (Use a strength to answer this and report it as a weakness. For example, if you like to get a job done without procrastinating, state you are impatient at times because you like to get your work out on schedule. Or you might indicate that you are a perfectionist and that you will not release work until it is perfect.)
- What do you consider your greatest achievement?
- What do you do when two priorities compete for your time?
- What skills do you have that you feel need strengthening?
- Do you enjoy working alone or with other people? What courses did you like best in school?
- Your resume shows several short-term jobs. Could you explain?
- Your resume indicates several part-time positions while you were going to school. Do you believe these work experiences helped you as an individual? How?
- Why did you leave your last job?
- In selecting your career, did you consider the ease with which you absorbed knowledge in certain subjects? How?
- Why should we consider you for the job? Usually we hire someone with more experience than you have to offer.
- How can you make a contribution to our company?
- What do you know about our company?

Preparing supplies. A few days before the scheduled interview, prepare a list of everything you must do or take with you. Place in your briefcase your social security card, several copies of your resume, a list of references, several pens and sharpened pencils, a school transcript, and any personal work you would like to show the interviewer. On an index card, you should list facts about the company. You might wish to refer to them during your trip to the interview. Undoubtedly, you, too, will have questions for the interviewer. Jot them down on a card so that you don't fail to ask them.

The application. When you come to the interview, you might be asked to complete an application form. Use the information from your resume as you respond to the questions. Use a pen, write legibly, and respond to every question. If a question does not pertain to you, indicate that you read this question by responding with "NA," meaning not applicable.

During the Interview

Interviewers begin to evaluate candidates for jobs from the moment they read application letters and resumes or interview the job seeker, whichever is first. On written documents, interviewers look for appearance, arrangement, creativity in writing, initiative, and content. Your measurable skills and aptitudes are given in the resume; therefore, the interviewer determines from this document whether your skills meet the requirements of the position.

However, equally important are the intangible skills and personal qualities that come across during the interview. How do you communicate ideas in speaking? Do you have your own opinions? Do you ask questions if you need clarification of a statement? Do you listen attentively? Do you establish eye contact? Do you communicate a positive attitude? Factors used to evaluate a prospective employee are personality, maturity, motivation, flexibility, and enthusiasm. In secretarial careers, personal traits and qualifications are essential for success, especially in view of the constantly changing nature of the office, society, and business.

After the Interview

Be certain to thank the interviewer by name for having taken time to see you. If the interviewer doesn't indicate when a decision will be made, suggest that you will call on a certain day to find out if an applicant has been selected for the job.

Follow up the interview with a thank-you note in which you express your interest in the job and the opportunity to work for the company.

Each interview you have should be a learning experience and should lead to more self-confidence. So, don't fret if you don't get the job. Rather, think positively and apply what you learned from the first interview to the next one. Reassure yourself that you are the best qualified candidate for the job.

You might wish to maintain a record of your contacts so that you don't make the mistake of responding to the same help-wanted advertisement more than once. A sample form you might develop is shown in Figure 9.4.

ONCE YOU HAVE A JOB

You will want to keep your job search records on file, even after you have your job, because they represent an ongoing record of business contacts that you will enlarge and use many times during your career. Discard duplicate papers—you only need one good list of the names and addresses and company titles—and keep your file orderly and updated.

Networking means developing business contacts that will keep you in touch with many segments of your industry. By becoming a member of professional associations, by maintaining your contacts with people in your business field, you will learn a great deal. You will also find that, as you gain experience, you will have more and more opportunity to contribute to your field in a professional capacity. In the beginning, you can volunteer to help with simple tasks in your professional organization by doing mailings, gathering news for the monthly bulletin, or making phone calls for special campaigns. Later, as you learn more about your field, you may want to help with programs, lead panel discussions, report on changes in your industry, or hold an office.

Enriching Your Professional Life Is Up to You

There are endless possibilities, and you will discover more and more of these as you go along. Talk with the other people in the office where

Figure 9.4 RECORD OF EMPLOYER CONTACT

Company Name, Address, and Phone	Application Letter Mailed	Resume Mailed (via post office or e-mail)	Date of Interview (telephone, computer, or face-to-face)	Name of Interviewer	Thank-you Note	Follow-up Letter	Offer Received	Rejection Received
Business Systems One Olga Drive Clifton, NJ, 20363-5408 Phone: (201) 555-3600					April 26	May 10	May 11	No.

you get your job. Learn to be a good coworker, and a good friend, by being tactful, useful, and reliable, on the job. Your coworkers can be helpful in letting you know the expectations of the department, the office style in the little things like who usually takes care of social plans such as birthday lunches and holiday gift exchanges. These are small parts of each working day that you will want to participate in and enjoy with the rest of the office staff. They provide good opportunities for you to get to know the others and to hear from them in an informal way many of the other small details that make up the fabric of office life. By being a good listener, you will be able to learn a good deal that will help you get along well and make a place for yourself in the new group.

Continuing education, whether on-the-job or in a school evenings or weekends, plus the contacts at work and in professional associations will help to enrich your professional life. They will help to provide knowledge and contacts that will assist you when you consider a job change, promotion, or expansion of your duties. Secretarial careers can carry you to a great variety of challenging roles in many kinds of work, and with care, your career can be a satisfying, many-sided adventure.